Eugene O'Neill

POEMS

1912–1944

Edited by Donald Gallup

New Haven and New York

TICKNOR & FIELDS

1980

Library of Congress Cataloging in Publication Data

O'Neill, Eugene Gladstone, 1888–1953.
  Poems, 1912–1944.

  Includes index.
  I. Gallup, Donald Clifford, 1913–
PS3529.N5A17 1980   811'.52   79–28066
ISBN 0–89919–007–3

Printed in the United States of America

V 10 9 8 7 6 5 4 3 2 1

Dedicated to the Memory of
Carlotta Monterey O'Neill
(28 December 1888–17 November 1970)

INTRODUCTORY NOTE

The chief reason for the publication of this edition is to make available the serious poems Eugene O'Neill wrote between 1915 and 1917, in 1925, and in 1942. Manuscripts or typescripts of these in the O'Neill collection at Yale were given by the O'Neills, but with the stipulation that they were not to be made available to scholars. Carlotta Monterey O'Neill, after the death of Eugene O'Neill in 1953, continued the restriction, and asked that it be applied also to the typescripts acquired by Yale in 1966 from Agnes Boulton, but did make an exception in favor of William H. Davenport, whose article "The Published and Unpublished Poems of Eugene O'Neill" was printed in the *Yale University Library Gazette* for October 1963. Mr. Davenport, at the end of his discussion of the poems, ventured the guess that "Someday, perhaps, a collected edition of the materials . . . may yet see the light."

And, indeed, it has seemed best not to limit the present publication to just the more interesting poems of which manuscripts and typescripts happen to exist at Yale, but to include all the known published poems and as many unpublished ones as could easily be located. (Other early love poems exist, addressed to Maibelle Scott and others.) We are grateful to the Henry W. and Albert Berg Collection, the New York Public Library, Astor, Lenox and Tilden Foundations, for permission to print manuscript or typescript poems in the Berg Collection, and to Clifton Waller Barrett and the University of Virginia Library for authorization to publish manuscript poems at Virginia.

Beyond the appearance of individual poems in periodicals and newspapers, the only considerable prior publication of O'Neill's verse was in the Sanborn and Clark *Bibliography* in 1931. There thirty of the poems were reprinted—twenty-six of them from the *New London Telegraph*—prefaced by "An Explanation":

> The reader is requested to remember that the following poems are examples of Mr. O'Neill's earliest work and that he was extremely reluctant to have them reprinted. However, he has graciously given his consent in order that this record might be complete.

There is further documentation of Eugene O'Neill's attitude toward the *Telegraph* poems in the proofs—now at Yale—of Barrett Clark's *Eugene O'Neill* (1929), which Clark submitted to O'Neill for his approval. Besides reprinting "It's Great When You Get In" (from the *Telegraph*) in its entirety, Clark had, in the proofs, written at greater length than in the book as published about the poems, quoting a stanza each of "Nocturne" and "Only You." Deleting these passages, O'Neill wrote in the margin:

> I wish you would leave all this out. . . . The seriousness with which you take it, the amount of space you give it, all serve to create a wrong impression of my own opinion of it—now and in those days. . . . To me it seems this stuff had no bearing on my later development. I never submitted a verse that was really close to me, that I had felt, to the Telegraph. I couldn't—and unless you understand this about me at that time—as now—you've got me wrong!
>
> . . . I was trying to write popular humorous journalistic verse for a small town paper and the stuff should be judged—nearly all of it—by that intent.

His opinion of the early verse had not changed seven years later when, in 1936, Francesco Bianco, an uncle by marriage of Agnes Boulton, suggested a separate edition of the poems. O'Neill replied (on 3 February):*

> Frankly . . . I am all against it. It would be a shame to waste good type on such nonsense. If those small-town jingles of my well-misspent youth were amusingly bad, I would have no objection, for their republication might hand someone a laugh, at least. But they're not. They are merely very dull stuff indeed—and so my decision must be to let them lie suitably defunct.

    . . .

*I am indebted to Louis Sheaffer for calling my attention to this letter and for supplying a photocopy of it. —Ed.

I appreciate your kindness in offering to return the clippings. Yes, I would like to have them—for that's about the only value they can possibly have for anyone—their value to me, as keepsakes of old times.

As Barrett Clark pointed out,

Every one of . . . [the early poems] is an imitation of or parody on some writer. The chief influences I detected were Kipling and Villon, and the best parodies were on Walt Mason, [Robert] Burns and [Robert W.] Service.

For a few of the poems, O'Neill himself indicated the sources of his inspiration; in this edition the notes point out some, but by no means all, of the others. The notes give also the publication history, so far as it is known, of each poem. Since, where variant versions of poems exist, it is possible to be certain of the text O'Neill regarded as final, that version has generally been used. (In one or two instances important variations between earlier and final texts are given in the notes.) Misprints and spelling errors, including O'Neill's frequent, characteristic use of the apostrophe in the possessive form of the neuter third-person pronoun, his occasional omission of the apostrophe in the possessive form of nouns, and his habitual misspelling "rythm," have been silently corrected. Titles are given set uniformly in capital letters without full stops.

The editor gratefully acknowledges his indebtedness to Dr. Lola Szladits and the Berg Collection's staff, to Mrs. Joan St. C. Crane of the University of Virginia Library, to Mrs. Whitten of the New London Public Library, to Dr. Virginia Floyd, and to Louis Sheaffer for much valued help.

A preliminary edition of these poems (made possible by a grant from the Witter Bynner Memorial Foundation for Poetry) was issued by the Yale University Library for private circulation in 1979 as *Poems 1912–1942*. Grateful acknowledgment is made to the Collection of American Literature, Beinecke Rare Book and Manuscript Library, to the Yale University Library, and to Yale University (as legatee under the will of Carlotta Monterey O'Neill) for permission to print this edition.

1. FREE

Weary am I of the tumult, sick of the staring crowd,
Pining for wild sea places where the soul may think aloud.
Fled is the glamour of cities, dead as the ghost of a dream,
While I pine anew for the tint of blue on the breast
    of the old Gulf Stream.

I have had my dance with Folly, nor do I shirk the blame;
I have sipped the so-called Wine of Life and paid the price
    of shame;
But I know that I shall find surcease, the rest my spirit
    craves,
Where the rainbows play in the flying spray,
'Mid the keen salt kiss of the waves.

Then it's ho! for the plunging deck of a bark, the hoarse
    song of the crew,
With never a thought of those we left or what we are going
    to do;
Nor heed the old ship's burning, but break the shackles
    of care
And at last be free, on the open sea, with the trade wind
    in our hair.

First published in the *Pleiades Club Year Book* ([New York, Pleiades Club, 1912]), p. 120, as by Eugene G. O'Neill; reprinted in *A Bibliography of the Works of Eugene O'Neill* by Ralph Sanborn and Barrett H. Clark (New York, Random House, 1931)—cited hereafter as Sanborn & Clark—pp. [111]-112. The O'Neill papers in the Collection of American Literature, Beinecke Rare Book and Manuscript Library, Yale University—cited hereafter as YCAL—include a typed copy of the poem made by Carlotta Montery O'Neill about 1940. Eugene O'Neill gave the autograph manuscript of this poem to Maibelle Scott. See Arthur and Barbara Gelb, *O'Neill* (New York, Harper & Brothers [1962])—hereafter referred to as Gelb, *O'Neill*—p. 210.

2. "FOR THE WATERWAYS CONVENTION'S IN THE MORNING"

(With apologies to Rudyard K[ipling]'s "Danny Deever")

"Why are the flags all hanging out?" said the cop
    on the Parade.
"To welcome them, to welcome them" the humble "white-wing"
    said.
"Why do you look so neat, so neat?" said the cop
    on the Parade.
"I've got to look my best today," the humble "white-wing"
    said.
"They have come from Pennsylvania, Georgia, Maine and
    Delaware,
Massachusetts and New Jersey; you can see them everywhere.
Every boarding house is crowded, not an inch of room
    to spare,
For the Waterways Convention's in the morning."

"What are the bands all playing for?" said the cop
    on the Parade.
"To cheer them up, to cheer them up," the humble "white-wing"
    said.
"Why are those lights across the street?" said the cop
    on the Parade.
"To give the town a festive look," the humble "white-wing"
    said.
"They have strung them over State street, from the top clear
    to the bay,
It will look just like a picture of a section of Broadway.
We will show them what it really is to turn night into day,
For the Waterways Convention's in the morning."

"They say the Beach is fixed up, too," said the cop
    on the Parade.
"You bet it is, you bet it is," the humble "white-wing"
    said.

"I fear I'll have my work cut out," said the cop
    on the Parade.
"No doubt you will, no doubt you will," the humble "white wing"
    said.
"For they've foundered all the taxis and they've swamped
    the trolley cars,
And you'll find them in the soda shops, and maybe in the bars.
Oh, we're due to think we've run into a hundred shooting stars,
When the Waterways Convention starts this morning."

"What is that awful noise I hear?" said the cop
    on the Parade.
"The speakers have begun, I guess," the humble "white-wing"
    said.
"Then we're going to have some speeches?" said the cop
    on the Parade.
"About a hundred thousand," the humble "white-wing" said.
"They will orate on the subject of our harbors, rivers,
    bays,
Using technical expressions in a thousand puzzling ways.
Oh, you can bet you'll find me sitting watching
    moving picture plays
When the Waterways Convention starts in speaking."

Printed, in the *New London Telegraph*, sometime before the Waterways Convention in New London, 3–4 September 1912, as by Eugene G. O'Neil [*sic*]. YCAL has an undated clipping, not identified as to source. A "white-wing" is a street-sweeper, wearing a white uniform.

3. THE WATERWAYS CONVENTION,
A STUDY IN PROPHECY

(With apologies to [Longfellow's] *Hiawatha*)

O the conning and the bulling!
O the bulling and the conning!
Those three golden days of summer,
When the Waterways Convention
Came at last to old New London.
Chieftains from far distant regions
Came to test our festal welcome,
Came and spoke, and then departed.
Spoke of what they knew, and often —
Wisely spoke of what they knew not.
O the welcome that we gave them!
How we tendered them the glad hand!
How we dined and even wined them!
Feasts and races and receptions!
Took the lid right off our prices.
Let them soar way up to heaven.
Saying sagely "For safe-keeping
You had better leave your wampum
In the city of New London."

Hitherward came Big Bill Taftus,
Chieftain of our mighty nation
Faint hope of the Grand Old Party
With an eye for snaring voters.
Big he was in point of body,
And his words were even bigger
When he spoke about the future
Of our dear old Whaling village.
Spoke about our glorious future
(With an eye for snaring voters).

4

Brothers we shall all remember
How before the whole convention
Gravely spoke our chief Mahanus,
Sachem of the tribe of Whalers,
Blessed with gift of divination
He removed the veil of Isis,
Peered into the misty future,
Sketched with rare prophetic sureness
The New London of the future.

"Thirty-story office buildings
We will see the length of State street.
We will take the "tube" to Groton
And the subway clear to Noank,
Or the "L" to Oswagatchie.
We will gather at the new docks
To see off the Lusitania.
And our bay will be so crowded
We will have a traffic policeman
Rowing beats upon the waters.
And we'll have an adding expert
To keep track of the collisions.

A Stock Exchange will be on Main street
And the Capital we'll pilfer
From the puny grasp of Hartford.
We will then produce our great men.
Envy not New York its Becker
We will have a greater grafter.
We will have our bands of "gun men"
"Gyp the Bloods" and "Lefty Louies"
And mayhap — the gods propitious —
We will even have a Thaw trial.
Property will rise in value

Till we're all so rich, my brothers,
That our heirs will try to slip some
Cyanide into our porridge."

Here the sachem of our city
Paused to make his words more weighty;
Quoth he "All we need is wampum
All we need is the dinero"
And at this the whole convention
Rose and shouted as one body
"All we all need is the wampum."

Printed, under the heading "Laconics," in the *New London Telegraph* for
26 August 1912, as by Eugene O'Neill; reprinted in Sanborn & Clark, pp.
121–123. The Waterways Convention delegates met in New London on 3
and 4 September 1912. Ex-Police Lieutenant Charles Becker and gun men
Harry ("Gyp the Blood") Horowitz and Louis ("Lefty Louie") Rosenberg
were involved in the murder in July 1912 of a gambler, Herman Rosen-
thal, who had been scheduled to testify in an investigation of police cor-
ruption in New York City gambling houses. Harry Kendall Thaw (1871–
1947) was first tried for the murder of Stanford White on 25 June 1906 and
found guilty; at the second trial on 6 January 1908 he was judged insane
and ordered confined to the Matteawan State Hospital.

4. VILLANELLE OF YE YOUNG POET'S FIRST VILLANELLE TO HIS LADYE AND YE DIFFICULTIES THEREOF

To sing the charms of Rosabelle,
To pour my soul out at her feet,
I try to write this villanelle.

Now I am caught within her spell,
It seems to me most wondrous sweet
To sing the charms of Rosabelle.

I seek in vain for words to tell
My love—Alas, my muse is weak!
I try to write this villanelle.

Would I had power to compel
The English language incomplete
To sing the charms of Rosabelle.

The ardent thoughts that in me dwell
On paper I would fair repeat
I try to write this villanelle.

My effort fruitless is. O H—l!
I'll tell her all when next we meet.
To sing the charms of Rosabelle,
I tried to write this villanelle.

Printed, under the heading "Laconics," in the *New London Telegraph* for 27 August 1912, as by Eugene O'Neill; reprinted in Sanborn & Clark, p. 124. The poem was written for Maibelle Scott.

5. BALLAD[E] OF OLD GIRLS

Where is Cora the corn-fed girlie?
  Idol of mine in the bare-foot days,
Whose laughing summons awoke me early
  To "hide and seek" in the woodland ways.
Where is the heroine of the plays?
  Who mocked my first calf-love, I fear;
Probably playing the "Four-a-days!"
  "But where are the snows of yester year?"

Where is Edith the prep-school beauty?
  Whose notes I found in a chink of the wall
Letters of love addressed to "Cutie"
  Answered by "Light of my soul," "My all"
Where is the "widow" of Nassau Hall?
  Always there with the college cheer,
Yours in springtime and mine in fall
  "But where are the snows of yester year?"

Where are Betty and Maud and Mabel?
  Chorus ladies that cared for wine,
With appetites o'erwhelmingly able,
  Leaving you skinned to a last lone dime
Where's May the queen of the burlesque "time"?
  Not averse to a schooner of beer,
Tipping the scales at two hundred and nine,
  "But where are the snows of yester year?"

Let me not ask where they are gone
  Forgotten am I by them all I fear
The future calls with its witching song
  "But where are the snows of yester year?"

Printed, under the heading "Laconics," in the *New London Telegraph* for 28 August 1912, as by E. O.; reprinted in Sanborn & Clark, pp. 125–126, as "Ballard of Old Girls." For the refrain see François Villon's "Ballade des dames du temps jadis," translated by Dante Gabriel Rossetti as "Where are the snows of yesteryear?"

6.

(With apologies to J. W. Riley)

Our Teddy opens wide his mouth,
　　N'runs around n'yells all day,
N'calls some people naughty names,
　　N'says things that he shouldn't say.
N'when he's nothing else to do
　　He swells up like he'd like to bust,
N'pounds on something with his fist
　　N'tells us 'bout some wicked trust.
　　I always wondered why that was —
　　　　I guess it's 'cause
　　　　Taft never does.

He tells the farmers how to sow
　　N'shows the cav'lry how to ride,
N'if you try to say a word
　　He's angry, n'he says you lied.
N'when it's quiet over here
　　He goes way far acrost the seas
N'gets a great big gun n'shoots
　　The elephants n'chimpanzees.
　　I always wondered why that was —
　　　　I guess it's 'cause
　　　　Taft never does.

Printed, without title, under the heading "Laconics," in the *New London Telegraph* for 2 September 1912, as by Eugene O'Neill; reprinted in Sanborn & Clark, p. 127, and in Gelb, *O'Neill*, pp. 198–199. In the 1912 election, President William Howard Taft, Republican, ran against Progressive party candidate Theodore Roosevelt, of redoubtable fame as a big-game hunter, and Democrat Woodrow Wilson (who won).

7.

All night I lingered at the Beach
And trod the board walk up and down —
I vainly sought to cop a peach.

I had prepared a charming speech,
To woo the fair ones of the town —
All night I lingered at the Beach.

Quoth I "Sweet damsel I beseech
That you will smile on me," poor clown!
I vainly sought to cop a peach.

With the persistence of a leech,
I clung to every passing gown —
All night I lingered at the Beach.

I swore my love to all, but each
Passed me the haughty freezing frown —
I vainly sought to cop a peach.

I prayed to all, both white and brown —
They only "kicked my dog aroun."
All night I lingered at the Beach —
I vainly sought to cop a peach.

Printed, without title, under the heading "Laconics," in the *New London Telegraph* for 6 September 1912, as by E. O.; reprinted in Sanborn & Clark, p. 128.

8. TO A BULL MOOSE
(With apologies to Bobby Burns['s "To a Field Mouse"])

Braw, snortin', roarin', fearsome beastie
What a tumult's in thy breastie
Thou needna think that we will heed thee
    Or mark thy clatter
Thou canna make us believe we need thee
    By inane chatter.

Poor beastie, 'tis an ill opinion
To think we'd suffer thy dominion
Thy fate is sealed for next November
    After election
Then present boasts thou wilt remember
    With deep dejection.

So, Moosie, cease thy bragging vain
We canna hear thee wi'out pain
The best laid plans of Moose and men
    Gang aft agley
We can but hope that thine will wend
    The self-same way.

Printed, under the heading "Laconics," in the *New London Telegraph* for
11 September 1912, as by E. O.; reprinted in Sanborn & Clark, p. 129. A
"Bull Moose" was a member of the Progressive party, a follower of
Theodore Roosevelt.

9.

I might forget the subway guard
  Who said "Please watch your step" to me
The silent barber once I met
  Might e'en escape my memory
But I shall surely ne'er forget
  While breath of life is left in me
The waiter who urbanely said
  "I really can't accept a fee."

Printed, without title, under the heading "Laconics," in the *New London Telegraph* for 11 September 1912, as by E. O.; reprinted in Sanborn & Clark, p. 130.

10.

I used to ponder deeply o'er
The referendum and recall.
And culled statistics evermore
About the mighty tariff wall.

I followed every candidate,
Read their acceptance speeches, too,
And went to hear them all orate
'Bout what they would or wouldn't do.

As I have said, my thoughts flew high,
(They very rarely touched the ground.)
So that I was considered by
My friends as being most profound.

But truth will out; I must confess
At present I am in a fix.
Although my mind's uneasiness
Has naught to do with politics.

You tell me that the G. O. P.
Has cleaned up in the state of Maine?
Hush! hush! what matters it to me?
But say, who'll cop that opening game?

Will Wood last out? Will Marquard blow?
Is Matty still there with the science?
Can Speaker wallop Jeff. Tesreau?
In brief, which is it, Sox or Giants?

Printed, without title, under the heading "Laconics," in the *New London Telegraph* for 13 September 1912, as by E. G. O'Neill; reprinted in Sanborn & Clark, p. 131. Joe Wood and Tris Speaker played baseball for Boston in 1912; Rube Marquard, Christy Mathewson, and Jeff Tesreau were pitchers for New York. Boston won the eight-game series, played 8–16 October, four to three (the second game, tied after ten innings, was called because of darkness).

11. NOCTURNE

The sunset gun booms out in hollow roar
  Night breathes upon the waters of the bay
  The river lies, a symphony in grey,
Melting in shadow on the further shore.

A sullen coal barge tugs its anchor chain
  A shadow sinister, with one faint light
  Flickering wanly in the dim twilight,
It lies upon the harbor like a stain.

Silence. Then through the stillness rings
  The fretful echo of a seagull's scream,
  As if one cried who sees within a dream
Deep rooted sorrow in the heart of things.

The cry that Sorrow knows and would complain
  And impotently struggle to express —
  Some secret shame, some hidden bitterness —
Yet evermore must sing the same refrain.

Silence once more. The air seems in a swoon
  Beneath the heavens' thousand opening eyes
  While from the far horizon's edge arise
The first faint silvery tresses of the moon.

Printed, under the heading "Laconics," in the *New London Telegraph* for
13 September 1912, as by E. O'Neill; reprinted in Sanborn & Clark, p. 132.

12. BALLAD[E] OF THE MODERN MUSIC LOVER

I have tried to fall for the stuff of Mozart
  Handel, Haydn — a dozen or more
But I guess my ear isn't framed for "beaux arts"
  For I found them all a terrible bore.
  I suffered through concerts by the score
Orgies of music that shook the room
  Till my brain was sick and my head was sore
— But the joy of my heart is a ragtime tune.

I confess I'm fond of that Mendelssohn-rag
  But not of Liszt's Rhapsody Hungarian
Which sounds to me like a musical jag
  (You see I am but a rank barbarian).
  The long-haired high-brows call me "vulgarian"
When the "Great Big Beautiful Doll" I croon
  For I'm strong for the music that's real American
And the joy of my heart is a ragtime tune.

You can't swing in the maze of the Turkey Trot
  To the strains of a Chopin symphony
Or the horrible noise that Wagner wrote
  Or chaotic nocturnes of Tschaikowsky
  Such spasms are much too deep for me
And I pine mid the all-pervading gloom
  To hear that song 'bout the Robert E. Lee
For the joy of my heart is a ragtime tune.

            Envoy
High-brows, whom classic music quickeneth
  Heed well the burden of my vulgar rune,
Your lofty tumbling wearies me to death.
  The joy of my heart is a ragtime tune.

Printed, under the heading "Laconics," in the *New London Telegraph* for
17 September 1912, as by E. G. O'Neill; reprinted, as "Ballard of the

Modern Music Lover," in Sanborn & Clark, pp. 133–134. "Oh You Beautiful Doll," with words by A. Seymour Brown and music by Nat D. Ayer, was first published in 1911; "Waiting for the Robert E. Lee," with words by L. Wolfe Gilbert and music by Lewis F. Muir, was first published in 1912. The Turkey Trot was a popular dance step of the period.

In his comment on this poem in the proofs of his *Eugene O'Neill*, submitted for O'Neill's approval, Barrett Clark had stated: "I don't know whether O'Neill cares for music or not, but this Ballad seems to be the expression of an honest conviction." O'Neill wrote on the proof: "I did & do like good music — from my childhood — my mother was a fine pianist — exceptionally fine, I believe."

13.

As I scan the pages of history's scroll
  I find many scenes of woe,
And I read of the griefs that have griped the soul
  In the time of the long ago.
Of the tears and sobs at the Trojan gate,
  When the iron horse nosed in;
And the great despair of Alex. the Great
  With no more games to win.
And Caesar's thoughts were gloomy and dark
  When he piped that "Et tu Brute"
And the burning sensations of Joan of Arc,
  Were doubtless most acute.
I can sympathize with King Louis too
  As he stood on the guillotine,
And Napoleon's feelings at Waterloo
  When the Prussian host was seen.

I grant you their sorrows were great and real
  But comparison makes them light
With the gloom I feel as I ride my wheel
  To work on a Sunday night.

Printed, without title, under the heading "Laconics," in the *New London Telegraph* for 23 September 1912, as by E. O'Neill; reprinted in Sanborn & Clark, p. 135.

14. ONLY YOU

We walk down the crowded city street
  Thus, silently side by side
We loiter where mirth and misery meet
  In an ever refluent tide.

You thrill with the joy of the passing throng
  Or echo its weary sighs
You gaze at each face as it hurries along
  —But I only see your eyes—

I only see your eyes, my love,
  I only see your eyes
For happiness or misery
  Are only real when seen by me
Reflected in your eyes.

We walk down the crowded city street
  Lingeringly, side by side
You throb with the city's ceaseless beat
  While I in a dream abide.

For how can its harsh triumphant din
  Make me shudder or rejoice?
When the only sound in the dream I'm in
  Is the music of your voice.

The music of your voice, my love
  The music of your voice.
The world's vibrating symphony
  Seems vague and most unreal to me
I only hear your voice.

Written for Maibelle Scott. Printed, under the heading "Laconics," in the *New London Telegraph* for 27 September 1912, as by E. G. O'Neill; reprinted in Sanborn & Clark, pp. 136–137, and in Gelb, *O'Neill*, pp. 210–211.

15. "IT'S GREAT WHEN YOU GET IN"

They told me the water was lovely,
   That I ought to go for a swim,
The air was maybe a trifle cool,
   "You won't mind it when you get in"
So I journeyed cheerfully beach-ward,
   And nobody put me wise,
But everyone boosted my courage
   With an earful of jovial lies.

The Sound looked cold and clammy,
   The water seemed chilly and gray,
But I hastened into my bathing suit
   And floundered into the spray.
Believe me, the moment I touched it
   I realized then and there,
That the fretful sea was not meant for me
   But fixed for a polar bear.

I didn't swim for distance
   I didn't do the crawl,
(They asked why I failed to reach the raft,
   And I told them to hire a hall.)
But I girded my icy garments
   Round my quaking limbs so blue,
And I beat it back to the bath house
   To warm up for an age or two.

I felt like a frozen mummy
   In an icy winding sheet.
It took me over an hour
   To calm my chattering teeth.
And I sympathized with Peary,
   I wept for Amundsen's woes,

As I tried to awaken some life in
My still unconscious toes.

So be warned by my example
And shun the flowing sea,
When the chill winds of September
Blow sad and drearily.
Heed not the tempters' chatter
Pass them the skeptics' grin
For the greatest bull that a boob can pull
Is "It's great when you get in."

Printed, under the heading "Laconics," in the *New London Telegraph* for
28 September 1912, as by E. G. O'Neill; reprinted in Barrett H. Clark's
Eugene O'Neill (New York, R. M. McBride & Co., 1929), pp. 63–64. Roald
Amundsen (1872–1928) discovered the South Pole in December 1911;
Robert E. Peary (1856–1920) reached the North Pole on 6 April 1909.

16. THE SHUT-EYE CANDIDATE

(W[ith]. A[pologies]. to Rudyard Kipling['s "Tommy"])

Sez the wily campaign manager
  To the Corporations' man,
"Our candidate has gone dead broke,
  So help him if you can.
For the tour is long and the speeches strong
  And travelling comes high,
And we'll have to gather the coin in
  In order to get by."

Then it's "Graft! ! ! What graft?," we can't see
   anything wrong,
  Standard Oil and U.S. Steel, but candidate shut your eye;
And it's "Pass! All's well!" as the coin rolls along,
  You'll need an affidavit pretty badly by-and-by.

"It's private cars on the railroads
  A'roaming the country wide,
It's hotel bills and other ills
  And a helluvalot beside.
Don't throw your chip in boldly
  Be as cagey as you can,
For our candidate, be it understood,
  Is a conscientious man."

Then it's "Graft! What graft?" as we gather up the tin,
  Swift, Cudahy and Armour, O candidate shut your eye,
And it's "Pass! All's well!" as the old long green comes in,
  But you'll need an affidavit pretty badly by-and-by.

Printed, under the heading "Laconics," in the *New London Telegraph* for 3
October 1912, as by Eugene O'Neill; reprinted in Sanborn & Clark, pp.
138–139. New London's 1912 city election was held on 7 October.

21

17.   LOVE'S LAMENT
(Tigean Te Oa'Neill)

There ain't no nothing much no more,
  And nothin' ain't no use to me;
In vain I pace the lonely shore,
  For I have saw the last of thee.

I seen a ship upon the deep
  And signaled this here fond lament:
"I haven't did a thing but weep
  Since thou hast went."

Alas! fur I ain't one of they,
  What hasn't got no faith in love.
And them fond words of yesterday
  They was spoke true, by heaven above!

Is it all off twixt I and you?
  Will you go and wed some other gent?
The things I done, I'd fain undo,
  Since thou hast went.

O love! I done what I have did,
  Without no thought of no offense —
Return, return, I sadly bid
  Before my feelings get intense.

I have gave up all wealth and show
  I have gave up all thought of fame,
But, oh! what joy 'twould be to know
  That thou hadst came!

Printed, under the heading "Laconics," in the *New London Telegraph* for 6
October 1912, as "(Contributed.)"; reprinted in Sanborn & Clark, pp.
140–141, and in Gelb, *O'Neill*, p. 217.

18. "THE QUEST OF THE GOLDEN GIRL"

I wandered the wide world over and lingered in many a land in vain appeal for my great ideal, the girl who could understand. I looked over the queens of Paris, of London and Berlin too, but they simply couldn't get hep to me so I beat it over the blue. I made mad love to an Esquimau as we froze on the bergs of Svork, and earned headaches at Irish wakes a'courting colleens in Cork. I tied up with a South Sea Islander, but little hampered by clothes, and fell for a peach in Somaliland with a shin bone through her nose. I sauntered through South America from Caracas to the Horn. Most passionate flames were the Latin dames and I barely weathered the storm. I snared the fairy Geisha in tea rooms of Tokio and a slant-eyed "Chink" was the next I think fell a victim to Cupid's bow. My next was a Moro damsel who called me the "soul of her life" but I blew in fear 'cause the little dear was so handy with her knife. I followed my quest to Africa from Cairo to the Cape, squeezed many a hand in many a land with many a narrow escape. Ever the heart of me hungered, till I suddenly ceased to roam, and stowed away one lonely day on a boat that sailed for home. And there I finally met her and asked her to be my wife, and she understood as I knew she would the cause of my yearning strife. She revealed to me my longing in words no one could shirk when she said "My dear, my income's clear and you won't have to work."

Written in imitation of the prose poems of Walt Mason and printed, under the heading "Laconics," in the *New London Telegraph* for 17 October 1912, as by E. G. O'Neill; reprinted in Sanborn & Clark, p. 142.

19. THE GLINTS OF THEM

Laughing, gift laden did they come to me,
Their hands made fair with wondrous silver hours,
Their hair encrowned with wreaths of memory,
Light loves of old, as fragile as the flowers
Star-dotted in the gloom of woodland ways—
  Gold summer days.

The drowsy heated noontide revery;
Fantastic dreams beneath the lonely moon;
The weary sobbing rhythm of the sea,
Sighing its even melancholy rune;
The sand that shudders in the sun's hot rays—
  Gold summer days.

The bright, green lawns that lean down to the bay;
The dancing, eerie heat-waves on the road;
Cool shade wherein my listless feet would stray
Beneath great trees, the lovely nymph's abode
Or haunted by the fairy ghosts of fays—
  Gold summer days.

The sullen vessel straining at the chain;
The pungent smell of oily pitch and tow;
A vista of strange lands seen once again,
A breath of memory from the long ago;
The longing song of fortune's castaways—
  Gold summer days.

Printed, under the heading "Laconics," in the *New London Telegraph* for
19 October 1912, as by E. G. O'Neill; reprinted in Sanborn & Clark, p.143.

20. HITTING THE PIPE

"When my dreams come true—when my dreams come
true—I shall lean out from my casement in the
starlight and the dew" —J. W. Riley

When my dreams come true—when my dreams come true—
I'll be sitting in the office here with nothing else to do
But to write a comic story or to spin a little rhyme,
I won't have to do rewriting, I'll have lots of leisure time
For to sit and chatter politics and dream the whole night
 through,
I will never cover socials when my dreams come true!

When my dreams come true I will never stoop to read
The proof of advertisements telling people what they need.
I will only write the stories that are sure to make a hit,
And the mighty city editor will never cut a bit,
But put them in just as they are and compliment me, too,
I'll be the star reporter when my dreams come true.

When my dreams come true there will not be a mistake
In a single line of copy that the linotypers make
I will never have to count the letters framing up a head
And every night at twelve o'clock will find me home in bed
I will shun the railroad station and the police station, too,
And only cover prize fights when my dreams come true.

When my dreams come true all my comments wise and sage
Will be featured double column on the editor's own page
Personals will be no object, I won't have to go and hunt
The history of the tug boats that infest the water-front
Fire alarms may go to blazes, suicides and murders too,
I'll be editing Laconics, when my dreams come true.

Printed, under the heading "Laconics," in the *New London Telegraph* for
22 October 1912, as by E. G. O'Neill; reprinted in Sanborn & Clark, pp.
144–145, and in Gelb, *O'Neill*, p. 200.

21. SENTIMENTAL STUFF

I wrote a sonnet to her eyes,
  In terms Swinburnian and erotic;
Poured out the burden of my sighs
  With language lurid and exotic—
    She did not heed.

I wrote a ballad I deemed fair
  With sprithy play of silver rhyme
To sing her glorious golden hair
  Aglow with sun in summer time—
    She did not hear.

I wrote a soulful villanelle
  About the wonder of her mouth,
Lips like the crimson flowers that dwell
  In forests of the tropic south—
    She made no sign.

I wrote a musical rondeau
  To praise her roguish little nose,
Dabbed at with powder, white as snow,
  Through which a freckle warmly glows—
    She would not see.

I wrote a solemn, stately ode,
  Lauding her matchless symmetry,
I thought that this might be a road
  To open up her heart to me—
    She spoke no word.

Then in a feeble triolette,
  I told the keenness of her wit;
A blush of anger o'er me crept
  I was so much ashamed of it
    —She fell for it—

    —And this is it—
"What matters it if you are fair?
  I love you for your wit,
Your mental poise, your wisdom rare,
  What matters it if you are fair?
Beauty is fleeting, light as air
  I'll nought to do with it,
What matters it if you are fair?
  I love you for your wit."

She praised this assininity
  And scorned the good ones that I wrote,
This bunch of femininity,
  On whom my fond affections dote—
    Has got my goat.

She put my real ones on the pan,
And gave my puerile one a puff,
And said, "I'll love you if you'll can
  That horrid sentimental stuff—
    I've had enough."

Printed, under the heading "Laconics," in the *New London Telegraph* for 28 October 1912, as by E. G. O'Neill; reprinted in Sanborn & Clark, pp. 146–147.

22.   A REGULAR SORT OF A GUY

He fights where the fighting is thickest
  And keeps his high honor clean;
From finish to start, he is sturdy of heart,
  Shunning the petty and mean;
With his friends in their travail and sorrow,
  He is ever there to stand by,
And hark to their plea, for they all know that he
  Is a regular sort of a guy.

He cheers up the sinner repentant
  And sets him again on his feet;
He is there with a slap, and a pat on the back,
  For the lowliest bum on the street;
He smiles when the going is hardest,
  With a spirit no money can buy;
And take it from me, we all love him 'cause he
  Is a regular sort of a guy.

I don't care for the praise of the nations,
  Or a niche in the great hall of fame,
Or that posterity should remember me
  When my dust and the dust are the same;
But my soul will be glad if my friends say
  As they turn from my bier with a sigh
"Though he left no great name, yet he played out the game
  Like a regular sort of a guy."

Printed, under the heading "Laconics," in the *New London Telegraph* for 4
November 1912, as by E. G. O'Neill; reprinted in Sanborn & Clark, p.148.

23. THE LONG TALE

(With apologies to R[udyard]. K[ipling's "The Long Trail"].)

There's a speech within the hall, echoes back from wall
    to wall,
    Where the campaign banners swing;
And the voters sit so patient, listening to the tale
    so ancient,
    That the old spellbinders sing.
You have heard the story of thieving Trusts
    And their lawless lust for gain;
You have heard that song — how long! how long?
    'Tis the same old tale again!
We have fallen for that same bull, dear lass,
    Many a season through,
Till we're getting fed up with the old tale, the cold tale,
    thrice-told tale
Yes, we're just about sick of that Long Tale, the tale
    that is never new.

It's North you may run to Seattle, Washington,
    Or South to the Florida strait;
Or East all the way to Massachusetts Bay,
    Or West to the Golden Gate;
And the greatest bluffs hold good, dear lass,
    And the wildest tale seems true,
And the men talk big on the old tale, the cold tale,
    thrice-told tale
Yes, lies run large on the Long Tale, the tale
    that is never new.

The voters are grown cold, and the campaign's growing old,
    And the speakers shout o'er the land;

Every candidate will bust every blooming wicked Trust,
    At least, so we're made to understand.
For election's drawing near, dear lass,
    And the orator's face is blue.
So harken again to the old tale, the cold tale,
        thrice-told tale.
Yes, try to believe in the Long Tale, the tale
        that is never new.

They must herd their flock of goats, they are looking
        for the votes,
    And they'll pledge you to the wide, blue sky;
They will throw out the corrupt, in a manner most abrupt,
    That is, if elected — bye and bye!
O, it's wonderful stuff to pull, dear lass,
    And almost believe in it too;
They can't be stopped on the old tale, the cold tale,
        thrice-told tale.
They're hard to beat on the Long Tale, the tale
        that is never new.

O the big parades at night, with the torches flying bright,
    And the brazen blare of the band;
When the voter walks and walks, and the speaker talks and talks,
    Placing his rivals on the pan;
And he's sure to spiel on the Trust, dear lass,
    That's a thing he can't fail to do,
When he opens his mouth for the old tale, the cold tale,
        thrice-told tale.
When he bangs his fist in the Long Tale, the tale
        that is never new.

O the murmur of the crowd, and the cheering long and loud,
    As the candidate's chest expands;

And our feelings nearly boil, as he bawls out Standard Oil,
   For crushing our freedom in its hands.
He is going to stop all that, dear lass,
   But just between me and you;
I've heard it before this old tale, the cold tale,
    thrice-told tale,
Yes, I've had an ear full of the Long Tale, the tale
    that is never new.

Yet before he turns to go, on the tariff high and low,
  He is sure to argue a while;
Let us not have a misgiving, he will lower cost of living,
   So he assures us with a smile.

You have heard the drool of the tariff wall,
   Which the robber Trusts maintain;
You have heard that song—how long! how long?
   He's telling the tale again!

Lord knows what he'd find to say, dear lass,
   And the Deuce knows what he would do
If he couldn't fall back on the old tale, the cold tale,
    thrice-told tale.
If he couldn't bull on the Long Tale, the tale
    that is never new.

Printed, above the heading "Laconics," in the *New London Telegraph* for 5
November 1912, as by Eugene Gladstone O'Neill; reprinted in Sanborn
& Clark, pp. 149–151.

24. THE CALL

I have eaten my share of "stock fish"
  On a steel Norwegian bark;
With hands gripped hard to the royal yard
  I have swung through the rain and the dark.
I have hauled upon the braces
  And bawled the chanty song,
And the clutch of the wheel had a friendly feel,
  And the Trade Wind's kiss was strong.

So it's back to the sea, my brothers,
  Back again to the sea.
I'm keen to land on a foreign strand
  Back again to the sea.

I have worked with a chipping hammer
  And starved on a lime-juice tramp.
While she plunged and rolled, I have cleaned the hold
  Or coughed in the bilges damp.
I have sweated a turn at trimming,
  And faced the stoke hold's hell,
And strained my ear in attempt to hear
  The relieving watch's bell.

So it's back to the sea, my brothers,
  Back again to the sea.
And where I'll go, I don't quite know —
  Just back again to the sea.

For it's grand to lie on the hatches
  In the glowing tropic night
When the sky is clear and the stars seem near
  And the wake is a trail of light.

And the old hulk rolls so softly
  On the swell of the southern sea
And the engines croon in a drowsy tune
  And the world is mystery!

So it's back to the sea, my brothers,
  Back again to the sea.
Where regrets are dead and blood runs red,
  Back again to the sea.

Then it's ho! for the moonlit beaches,
  Where the palm trees dip and sway,
And the noontide heat in the sleeping street
  Where the restless burros bray.
I can hear the bands on the plazas
  In towns of a far-off land,
And the words come strong of a deep sea song,
  "We're bound for the Rio Grande."

So it's back to the sea, my brothers,
  Back again to the sea.
Where white seas toss 'neath the Southern Cross,
  Back again to the sea.

I'm sick of the land and the landsmen
  And pining once more to roam,
For me there is rest on the long wave's crest
  Where the Red Gods make their home.
There's a star on the far horizon
  And a smell in the air that call,
And I cannot stay for I must obey
  So good-bye, good luck to you all!

So it's back to the sea, my brothers,
    Back again to the sea.
Hear the seagulls cry as the land lights die!
    Back again to the sea.

Printed, under the heading "Laconics," in the *New London Telegraph* for 19 November 1912, as by E. G. O'Neill; reprinted in Sanborn & Clark, pp. 152–154, and in Gelb, *O'Neill*, pp. 213–214. Compare John Masefield's "Sea Fever."

SONNETS

25. THE HAYMARKET

The music blares into a ragtime tune—
    The dancers whirl around the polished floor;
Each powdered face a set expression wore
    Of dull satiety, and wan smiles swoon
On rouged lips at sallies opportune
    Of maudlin youths whose sodden spirits soar
On drunken wings; while through the opening door
    A chilly blast sweeps like the breath of doom.

In a sleek dress suit an old man sits and leers
    With vulture mouth and blood-shot, beady eyes
At the young girl beside him. Drunken tears
    Fall down her painted face, and choking sighs
Shake her, as into his familiar ears
    She sobs her sad, sad history—and lies!

26. NOON

'Tis noon, the fitful sunlight feebly gleams
    Thro' hurrying clouds with dull uncertainty.
Distorted shadows in strange fantasy
    Play like vague phantoms wandering in dreams
Upon the shivering surface of the streams.
    The trees sway to and fro protestingly
Dancing as if to the weird melody
    Of anguished protest that the north wind screams.

The seer, dead leaves whirl in confusion by,
    Fleeing as if from nameless pestilence.

A solitary hawk up in the sky
Floats on the wind in peaceful indolence,
Like some old God, who from Olympus high
Looks on our dull world with indifference.

Printed, under the heading "Laconics," in the *New London Telegraph* for 21 November 1912, as by E. G. O'Neill; reprinted in Sanborn & Clark, pp. 155–156, and—"The Haymarket" only—in Louis Sheaffer, *O'Neill: Son and Playwright* (Boston, Toronto, Little, Brown and Co. [1968]), p.137.

27. BALLAD[E] OF THE SEAMY SIDE

Where is the lure of the life you sing?
  Let us consider the seamy side:
The fo'castle bunks and the bed bugs' sting,
  The food that no stomach could abide,
The crawling "salt horse" flung overside
  And the biscuits hard as a cannon ball;
What fascinations can such things hide?
  "They're part of the game and I loved it all."

Think of the dives on the water front
  And the drunken brutes in dungaree,
Of the low dance halls where the harpies hunt
  And the maudlin seaman so carelessly
Squanders the wages of months at sea
  And maybe is killed in a bar room brawl;
The spell of these things explain to me—
  "They're part of the game and I loved it all."

Tell me the lure of "working mail"
  With two hours' sleep out of twenty-four
Hefting bags huge as a cotton bale
  Weighing a hundred pounds or more,
Till your back is bent and your shoulders sore
  And you heed not the bosun's profane call;
Such work, I should think, you must abhor!
  "It's part of the game and I loved it all."

"I grant you the food is passing bad,
  And the labour great, and the wages small,
That the ways of a sailor on shore are mad
  But they're part of the game and I loved it all."

Printed, under the heading "Laconics," in the *New London Telegraph* for
22 November 1912, as by E. G. O'Neill; reprinted in Sanborn & Clark,
pp. 157–158, as "Ballard of the Seamy Side." A carbon typescript is among
the O'Neill papers (YCAL).

28. THE LAY OF THE SINGER'S FALL

A singer was born in a land of gold,
  In the time of the long ago
And the good fairies gathered from heath and wold
  With gracious gifts to bestow.
They gave him the grace of Mirth and Song,
  They crowned him with Health and Joy
And love for the Right and hate for the Wrong
  They instilled in the soul of the boy;
But when they were gone, through the open door
  The Devil of Doubt crept in,
And he breathed his poison in every pore
  Of the sleeping infant's skin,
And in impish glee, said "Remember me
  For I shall abide for aye with thee
From the very first moment thine eyes shall see
  And know the meaning of sin."

The singer became a man and he fought
  With the might of his pen and hand
To show for evil the cure long sought,
  And spread Truth over the land;
Till the Devil mockingly said, "In sooth
  'Tis a sorry ideal you ride,
For the truth of truths is there is no truth!"
  — And the faith of the singer died —

And the singer was sad and he turned to Love
  And the arms of his ladye faire,
He sang of her eyes as the stars above
  He sang of — and kissed — her hair;
Till the Devil whispered, "I fondly trust
  This is folly and nought beside,

For the greatest of loves is merely lust!"
  — And the heart of the singer died —

So the singer turned from the world's mad strife
  And he walked in the paths untrod,
And thrilled to the dream of a future life
  As he prayed to the most high God;
Till the Devil murmured with sneering breath,
  "What think you the blind skies hide?
There is nothing sure after death but death!"
  — And the soul of the singer died —

And the lips of the singer were flecked with red
  And torn with a bitter cry,
"When Truth and Love and God are dead
  It is time, full time, to die!"
And the Devil in triumph chuckled low,
  "There is always suicide,
It's the only logical thing I know."
  — And the life of the singer died.

Printed, under the heading "Laconics," in the *New London Telegraph* for
27 November 1912, as by E. G. O'Neill; reprinted in Sanborn & Clark,
pp. 159–160.

29. TO WINTER

"Blow, blow, thou winter wind."
  Away from here,
And I shall greet thy passing breath
  Without a tear.

I do not love thy snow and sleet
  Or icy floes;
When I must jump or stamp to warm
  My freezing toes.

For why should I be happy or
  E'en be merry,
In weather only fitted for
  Cook or Peary.

My eyes are red, my lips are blue
  My ears frost bitt'n;
Thy numbing kiss doth e'en extend
  Thro' my mitten.

I am cold, no matter how I warm
  Or clothe me;
O Winter, greater bards have sung
  I loathe thee!

Printed, under the heading "Laconics," in the *New London Telegraph* for 9
December 1912, as by E. G. O'Neill; reprinted in Sanborn & Clark, p.
161, and in Gelb, *O'Neill*, p. 222. "Cook" is Dr. Frederick A. Cook (1865–
1940), who reached the North Pole on 21 April 1908; Robert E. Peary
(1856–1920) reached it on 6 April 1909.

30. BALLADE OF THE BIRTHDAY OF THE MOST GRACIOUS OF LADYES

Lady accept this feeble rhyme;
  Pardon my lack of eloquence!
Fleshy weakness is more than mine
  Yet is my gratitude immense.
  Vainly in wrathful impotence
Writhes my spirit in speechless strife
  To put in words my wish intense—
Top of the morning and long life!

Hope's Hebe to the fever-toss'd!
  (Some figure of speech, you'll agree)
Kindest of bosses that e'er bossed!
  I'm almost glad to have T.B.
  Else I'd never have met you—see?
And real true friendship's none so rife,
  With all my heart I shout to thee—
Top of the morning and long life!

Angel of old pneumo-thorax!
  Fairy good with a temp-stick wand!
Bovine extract "sans" the borax
  Pour in the flagon in my hand!
  On almost unused legs I stand
And pound the table with my knife
  And shout (though it burst a T.B. gland)—
Top of the morning and long life!

Lady the parting of our ways
  Comes soon; yet back from out the strife
My heart will cry to all your days—
  Top of the morning and long life!

Written at the Gaylord Farm Sanatorium, Wallingford, Connecticut, 24 May 1913, to Mary A. Clark, nurse in charge of the infirmary. Printed from the autograph manuscript, signed and dated 24 May 1913, among the O'Neill papers (YCAL), which contain also a carbon typescript.

31. YE DISCONSOLATE POET TO HIS "KITTEN" ANENT YE BETTER FARM WHERE LOVE REIGNETH: BALLADE

List to the lure of my arguments,
   Harken awhile to the song I sing,
Fervent and fond are my sentiments,
   Ardent, indeed, is the love I bring.
Come to the land where love is king,
   (Meaning that Jersey farm of my sire;)
And scatter roses with wanton fling,
   Oh, come to my Land of Heart's Desire.

Lady, forget not we have T. B.
   Not our portion are endless years,
Then take what the present brings — that's me!
   Shun what the future hides — p'rhaps tears!
We'll match with Destiny for our "beers" —
   (To paraphrase Kipling I admire,)
Greet Mrs. Grundy with hoots and jeers,
   Oh, come to my Land of Heart's Desire.

Smile on my passionate plea abrupt,
   On bended (so to speak) knee I sue
Doubtless my morals are most corrupt,
   There is an elegant chance for you.
Why not reform my life? Thru and thru,
   Scour and cleanse my soul of the mire,
(A regular Christian thing to do)
   Oh, come to my Land of Heart's Desire.

Penance for sins we've paid in advance,
   T.B. is punishment full and dire,
Paid is the piper! On with the dance!
   Oh come to my Land of Heart's Desire!

Written for Katherine Murray, nurse, at the Gaylord Farm Sanatorium, Wallingford, Connecticut, in 1914. Printed from a manuscript (not in O'Neill's hand) in the Berg Collection of the New York Public Library.

32. FRATRICIDE

The call resounds on every hand,
　The loud, exultant call to arms
With patriotic blare of band
　It quickens, pulses, rouses, charms;
Mouthing its insolent command:
　"Come, let us rob our neighbors' farms."

Alas, what salve does conscience need
　When love of country's the pretense?
We must demand by force of deed
　The peon's scant remaining pence;
Nor see his misery, nor heed
　His wail of anguished impotence.

But who shall fight this holy war?
　Surely the servants of the great,
Those servile cringers at the door,
　Those parasites who fawn and wait,
Into whose clutching fingers pour
　The crumbs, the favors of the State.

Doubtless the bipeds of this breed
　Will be the first to join the hunt;
For lust of gold will fight and bleed,
　Will gladly bear the battle's brunt.
The cannon's hungry mouth will feed
　Upon them crowding to the front.

Ho, ho, my friend, and think you so?
　And have you not read history?
This much of war, at least, we know:
　The jingoes are the first to flee.
The plutocrats who cause the woe
　Are arrogant but cowardly.

They sow the wind, they watch it grow;
    With eager breath they fan the flame.
Fine indignation makes them glow.
    They rant about their country's fame.
They prate of liberty (you know
    That's part and parcel of the game).

But who is then the whirlwind's prey
    Since these foul curs turn tail and fly?
Who pays the price that some must pay?
    Whose widows mourn, whose orphans cry?
The poor! The poor who must obey,
    The poor who only live to die.

The army of the poor must fight,
    New taxes come to crush them down.
They feel the iron fist of Might
    Press on their brows the thorny crown.
They see the oily smile of Right.
    They don the sacrificial gown.

With ringing cheers they are led out,
    Poor sheep, to slay their brother sheep.
They are silent — only jingoes shout,
    And only wives and children weep.
What matter victory or rout
    So it brings on the final sleep!

Their shepherds bless them as they wait
    With unctuous platitudes inane.
With words of God instilling hate
    They slink off calling on his name
To polish the collection plate
    (For Christ was crucified in vain).

Scorched by the blazing tropic sun
  Some die of fever, some are shot.
In battles lost and battles won
  They give their lives and are forgot.
They die off slowly one by one.
  Their thin, unburied bodies rot.

At last a crowning victory;
  Then peace. Poor heroes all unnamed
The sad-eyed remnant home from sea
  Are cheered, and for a day are famed,
Then cast back into misery
  With weakened bodies sick and maimed.

For they must live and they must eat;
  Their families are hungry, too.
Back to the dark, foul-smelling street,
  The ruthless toil begins anew
Slave for a tainted bite of meat!
  The factory shambles claim their due.

Glory is weak, unwholesome fare
  For those who cry for lack of bread.
The war is over; who shall care
  If they be given stones instead?
With paltry pensions we shall dare
  To pay the women for their dead.

*   *   *

"A good war haloes any cause."
  What war could halo this cause, pray?
The wise man's words had given pause
  To him, were he alive today
To see by what unholy laws
  The plutocrats extend their sway.

What cause could be more asinine
    Than yours, ye slaves of bloody toil?
Is not your bravery sublime
    Beneath a tropic sun to broil
And bleed and groan—for Guggenheim!
    And give your lives for—Standard Oil!

Noble indeed to think your loot
    Is robbery of a brother's whole
Store of a lifetime. Brave, to boot
    To play the skulking butcher's role.
For every peon that you shoot
    A brother's death will stain your soul.

Go, tell the wan-faced, weeping wives
    The tale of your victorious war!
Gladden the lonely orphan lives
    With tales of smelters, wells galore!
Picture the happiness of Dives!—
    The poor are poorer than before.

Comrades, awaken to new birth!
    New values on the tables write!
What is your vaunted courage worth
    Unless you rise up in your might
And cry: "All workers on the earth
    Are brothers and WE WILL NOT FIGHT!"

Printed in the *New York Call* for 17 May 1914, as by Eugene G. O'Neill;
reprinted in Sanborn & Clark, pp. 113–117, and—four stanzas only—in
Gelb, *O'Neill*, p. 245.

33. A SONG OF MOODS
(to Bee)

When the sun sprites play on the laughing sea
     I cry to Thee.
When the mad leaves dance on the poplar tree
My glad heart sings to the winds of Thee —
     Ah, wantonly! So wantonly!
        Of Thee.

When the moonbeams dream on the sleeping sea
     I dream of Thee.
When the hushed leaves drowse on the poplar tree
My heart-throbs thrill through the night to Thee —
     Ah, tenderly! So tenderly!
        To Thee.

When the grey waves sulk on the sullen sea
     I sigh for Thee.
When the wan leaves weep on the poplar tree
My sad heart sobs in its need of Thee —
     Ah, longingly! So longingly!
       For Thee.

Written in New London in the summer of 1914 for Beatrice Ashe. Printed
from an original typescript among the O'Neill papers (YCAL). The words
"(to Bee)" after the title are in Eugene O'Neill's autograph and he has
added the place and date of composition. An earlier original typescript,
also among the O'Neill papers, differs chiefly in the order of the lines.
The O'Neill papers have also a manuscript copy of the earlier version of
the poem made by Carlotta Monterey O'Neill in 1954.

34. "UPON OUR BEACH"

Upon Our Beach we two lie, side by side—together!
Before us the sea, sparkling, vibrant with motion,
thrilling beneath the amorous sun's warm kisses.
Behind us a field of tough, wiry grass that waves
and ripples in wind-swept abandon.
Around and under us the hot sand glittering
with innumerable tiny jewels.
Above us a soft blue sky, the robe of the beneficent God
who blesses us.

There is a house on a distant hill, a cold, lonely,
ugly house, a millionaire's house.
The world would say this is his beach; he has a stamped
paper to prove it.
We know better,—and we have our hearts to prove it.
This is Our Beach!

We have felt it, caressed it, loved it together—and we,
in turn, know it loves us.
It is bound to us by tender cords of memory which only
that grim old hag with the shears shall ever sever.
Every wave, every blade of grass, every grain of sand
on this beach is attuned to us. We are familiar to them
and they to us.
What does he know of his beach, that food-stuffed adorer
of Mammon?
This is Our Beach!

There is nothing else to be seen to landward but a
far-off windmill, white against a clump of tall trees,
beautiful.

Away on the world's rim to seaward, hull-down, three or four sails, hazy, mysterious.

I watch them for a moment, dreaming, the mystery of the sea flooding me with vague longings, the Red Gods calling from their home on the horizon.

Vistas of strange lands float before my eyes — the docks at Buenos Aires, the avenidas, the race course at Palermo, the dives in Barracas.

I smell the bags of coffee being lowered into the hold. Santos, Bahia lie before me.

I see the harbor at Rio. I hear bands on the plazas and the rustle of the palm fronds. I remember my years of wandering in the tropics.

I remember my sailor days, — the pulling on ropes, the trick at the wheel, the lookout's sleepy call, the roll of a beam sea, the Southern Cross in the sky.

I see the faces, the honest, weather-beaten, good-natured, tanned faces of my mates in the forecastle.

The rollicking words of an obscene, old deep-sea chanty form on my lips — a chanty I last sang at anchor off the island of Trinidad.

(Trinidad! — the name conjures up cutlasses and pirates and pieces of eight.)

I smile to myself. Those mist-shrouded sails on the horizon might well be the ghosts of golden galleons of Spain.

For do they not bring me treasures of memories long dead, precious dreams of days of wonder?

Your hand moves slightly in the sand beside me. I come out of my dream with a start.

It is not often, Dear One, that thoughts in which you have no part ever occur to me.

You will pardon me this one time, will you not, My Beloved?

My glance is caught by the movement of a figure on a ledge of rocks jutting into the sea from the beach to the right of us.

I am surprised, startled. I had thought there was no living thing near us.

(I had forgotten the wheeling, sun-drunk seagull uttering at intervals its doleful cry — as if it were complaining about some deep-rooted sorrow in the heart of things.)

I study with an illogical interest the figure on the rocks.

It is an old bent man with a faded crimson jersey and trousers tucked into his sea-boots.

He casts a line into the sea; then waits patiently, wearily. He is fishing.

There is no joy, no life in any of his movements, — only an infinite sense of eternal repetition. He is blind to the beauty and leap of life around him.

He is not fishing for sport but because he wishes to eat.

(When life becomes a thing to be "worked out," why do men live? When there is no joy in the doing it is time to lay down one's tools.)

I turn away from the man. He has no part in my mood. Today, I cannot even pity him.

Today, I love life!

I turn to you, My Beloved. You are smiling at me. Your smile is tender and sweet. It sends a shiver of delight through me.

There is something of the pride of possession in your smile; yet my egotistic manhood is pleased, not offended by it.

Part of my highest dream is to be possessed by you. I desire nothing better than to belong to you, to be yours.

That you should proudly say to all the sneering world: "He is mine" — that also makes me proud.

For *you* are *mine*, are you not, My Beloved?

I meet your eyes. They are inscrutable, enigmatic, full of tenderness.

I would like to know what you are thinking of. If I asked you you would not tell me. Your evasions are also dear to me. They render you above all else feminine, charming.

I love your eyes. They are grey, green, flecked with golden lights. They are like the wind-kissed sea. They are like the sun-kissed sky.

And there is love for me in them. That is most wonderful of all. I see it there. I feel it.

A life of which you are part—Might not the Gods be justly jealous of it?

Today, I love life!

We are in each other's arms. We are kissing each other. Lip to lip and limb to limb we lie.

It is indiscreet. That dreary old fisherman might turn around. But what do Love and Youth care for Mrs. Grundys and life-sick old fishermen?

Your body clings to mine,—your beautiful body firm and supple as a tigress'. (There is sometimes a tigerish fierceness in you which I have noticed. I love you for it.)

Our kisses redouble. They are fire. I see your face dimly through quivering half-closed lids. I murmur half-choked words or sobs of tenderness. The world is a great rose-colored flame of desire.

Upon Our Beach we two lie side by side—together! Love and Youth are our only companions. Today, I love life.

I lean on my elbow beside you and gaze down upon you.

You have taken off your bathing cap and your dark hair hangs about your head in wind-tossed disarray.

Moved by a sudden impulse I must kiss you through it.

Ah, My Beloved, Love is sweet, is it not?

Your lips are soft, warm, red, like the rose petals of
Omar. I could sigh my life out on them.

You have white teeth. Your laugh is fun-loving,
kiss-provoking. Your nose is adorable.

I am glad the sun has also kissed your cheeks, your arms,
your neck. He, alone, I am not jealous of. I love him too much
myself, that fierce old lover.

There is a purple kiss upon your neck (necessitating much
concealment). I am sorry; but it is your fault indeed. Why
are you so sweet?

Your limbs are beautiful, your breasts are beautiful —
my lips yearn for them — your hips, your feet, your hands are
all beautiful.

I ache to possess you.

Today, I love life.

I lie beside you, half-naked, in my low-cut bathing suit.
I am brown and ugly. I feel like an ogre.

We form a fitting tableau — Beauty and the Beast!

Blind One, how can you love me? How is it possible?

Today, I love life!

A sudden bitterness floods my soul. I am thinking of the
long penance Necessity has put upon us. Alas, how long we must
wait for each other!

Alas, I am poor, too. How can you love me? I have none
of the virtues of a husband. I am a lover — in rags!

My future? Alas, how many broken ones have trusted in
tomorrows!

My spirits are at low ebb — so the low tide exposes on the
beach many dregs of the sea and writhing heaps of slimy
sea-weed.

I glance at the lonely house on the hill. I am envying
that over-stuffed one his riches. I am unworthy of your love.

You place your small hand caressingly upon my bare
shoulder. You guess my thoughts. You divine my depression.

I turn to you. Your eyes look into mine reproachfully. They chide me for my faint-heartedness, my lack of faith. They shine with loving confidence.

Exultant hope reawakens within me. With you beside me what abyss so deep as to affright me? What summit so high that I may not climb to it?

I thrill with new energy. Great aspirations arise within me. I build wonderful castles—fit dwelling places for us and our love.

I am one with the great restless spirit of sea and sun and sky and wind. I am part of the Great Purpose. I am Life— triumphant, unafraid, moving ever onward.

Out of the morass of my Despair have you pulled me with your little firm hand. Your eyes like the sea have restored to me my Highest Hope.

I must kiss you again, O lips like the rose petals of Omar.

Ah, My Beloved, Love is sweet, is it not?

Today, I love life!

Upon Our Beach we two lie side by side—together!

Love and Youth are our only companions.

Today, I love life!

Written in the summer of 1914 (before 22 September) for Beatrice Ashe. Printed from a carbon typescript in the Berg Collection of the New York Public Library. A manuscript note by Beatrice Ashe identifies the "millionaire's house" as the Harkness Hammond estates; the beach was on the property of Edward Crowninshield Hammond. See Louis Sheaffer, *O'Neill: Son and Playwright*, p. 283.

35. "FULL MANY A CUP OF THIS FORBIDDEN WINE"

The wan beams fret upon the shadowed floor
  As filmy cloud-wisps veil the wistful moon.
A silken curtain rustles in the gloom;
Sweet Summer breathes a kiss in thro' our door.
Vague, white, upon a chair the clothes you wore—
  And in the air your tangled hair's perfume;
And in my arms the body I adore!

Encircled by your supple limbs' unrest,
  Your warm sighs vagrant in my hair, I lie.
Won is the guerdon of my frenzied quest,—
  Love that endures, and joys which multiply.
Tonight my lips sleep on your bare soft breast,
  The beating of your heart their lullaby.

Written, probably in the summer of 1914, for Beatrice Ashe. Printed
from a carbon typescript among the O'Neill papers acquired from Agnes
Boulton (YCAL). That carbon and another carbon in the Berg Collection
of the New York Public Library have revisions.

36. "JUST A LITTLE LOVE, A LITTLE KISS"

Outside the rattling flat-wheeled cars roar by;
  The subway's rumbling clamor fills the air;
  The street's few wretched trees loom black and bare
Against the dreary murkiness of sky.

Cooped in this prison cell I call my room,
  Which goads me with its glaring sordidness,
  I drink the very dregs of bitterness,
I wander in abysmal depths of gloom.

A wan-faced woman with a ragged shawl
  Trundles a battered organ to the gate,
  Turning the crank, her sad eyes desolate,
Her music drowned beneath a newsboy's brawl.

She stands and shivers, and her eyes beseech
  The pennies which will buy her food and bed.
  Her sad old tune whines slowly through my head
Calling the Past.—I see a wave-swept beach.

A ledge of rocks that juts into the sea;
  The swift gulls dip, I hear their fretful cry;
  Far off the white sails of the ships glide by;—
I sit and dream,—and You are close to me.

My arms are round you; so we sit and dream
  And kiss and dream again, and smile and sigh;
  Say and do foolish things and question why;
Then laugh and kiss again and sigh and dream.

O Love of Mine, My Own, My Heart's Desire,
   I love you so, I want you, need you so!
   How vain are words to speak the love I know!
How hollow sound the tinklings of my lyre!

"Summer, indeed, is gone with all his rose"?
   Ah, but the soul of Summer haunts me yet,
   Conjured by this refrain, I can't forget, —
A song you sang at one soft twilight's close.

That quavering music by fond Memory's grace
   Summons your living beauty from the air,
   The magic of your eyes, your wind-tossed hair,
The wonder and the sweetness of your face.

The music stops. I watch the woman go.
   I hear the city's growling monotone.
   The spell has fled. I am alone, alone!
And oh, My Love, I want you, need you so!

Written 9 January 1915 and sent to Beatrice Ashe. (The title refers to a song she sang, "A Little Love A Little Kiss," words by Adrian Ross, music by Lao Silesu, published in 1912.) Printed from a carbon typescript among the O'Neill papers acquired from Agnes Boulton (YCAL). Both the carbon and the original typescript in the Berg Collection of the New York Public Library have autograph corrections by the author.

37. "JUST ME N' YOU"
(From a child to a child)

We're outward bound for the Land of Dreams, —
    Just me n'you.
Our course set by a star that gleams
    For me n'you.
We've nailed our hope-flag to the mast,
Set sail and left behind the Past,
We know we'll reach our port at last, —
    Just me n'you.

We're heading for the Land of Spain, —
    Just me n'you.
You bet we won't come back again, —
    Not me n'you.
We'll stay where hearts may keep the Spring,
Where Love rules over everything,
Where all the birds are glad to sing
    To me n'you.

There won't be no one there at all
    But me n'you.
In summer, winter, spring or fall, —
    Just me n'you.
Of course the home folk all will grin
And mock as jealously as sin,
But we will never care a pin, —
    Not me n'you.

We'll build our castle by the sea, —
    Just me n'you.
Upon our beach we'll wander free, —
    Just me n'you.

And then, and then—just think of this!—
We'll kiss, n'kiss, n'kiss, n'kiss,
N'kiss, n'kiss, *and* hug n'kiss,—
    Just me n'you.

Oh, that'll be a happy time
    For me n'you.
When all of life'll be in rhyme
    For me n'you.
Though God now seems to hesitate,
The days move at so slow a rate,
We know He'll pay us for our wait,—
    Just me n'you.

    Just me n'you,
    Just you n'me,
    Till life wake to
      Eternity!

Written 10 January 1915 and sent to Beatrice Ashe. Printed from a carbon typescript among the O'Neill papers acquired from Agnes Boulton (YCAL). Both the carbon and the original typescript in the Berg Collection of the New York Public Library have minor corrections in typing.

38. "BALLADE OF THE TWO OF US"

When our dreams come true,
   As we hope they may;
When the skies are blue,
   And the clouds astray,
   We shall laugh and play
As God's children do;
   Put the world away, —
Just I and You.

I shall kneel and sue
   And adore alway.
I shall think up new
   Sweet prayers to pray.
   In a different way
I shall come to woo,
   When we win our day; —
Just I and You.

Love is ever new
   When it's always May;
When there's naught to rue
   In dead yesterday;
   No goodbyes to say
Which will part us two.
   We'll kiss and be gay, —
Just I and You.

Let old Wealth delay,
   Fame ignore us too,
If our love but stay, —
   And I and You.

Written 11 January 1915 and sent to Beatrice Ashe. Compare James Whitcomb Riley's "When My Dreams Come True." Printed from the carbon typescript among the O'Neill papers acquired from Agnes Boulton (YCAL). Both the carbon and the original typescript in the Berg Collection of the New York Public Library give the year, erroneously, as 1910.

39. IMPRESSION

(Being a memory of Jan. 2rd [sic].)

Grey sky, and a road by the sea,
Lisp of waves on the drowsy air,
White snowflakes drifting downward listlessly.

You laugh, your alluring eyes gleam.
Hush, the weary earth is asleep.
Kiss softly lest we awake from our dream.

You are chasing the flakes of snow,
Red lips parted, your mouth upturned,
Sparkling-eyed, enticing, your face aglow.

Each snowflake elusively slips
Past your mouth; you catch one at last.
It melts in a kiss of our meeting lips.

No moan from the dreaming sea,
Drifting snow on the drowsy air,
O sleeping world, wake to our ecstasy!

Written 12 January 1915 and sent to Beatrice Ashe. Printed from the original typescript in the Berg Collection of the New York Public Library.

40. RONDEAU, TO HER NOSE

I wiped her nose! At her request
I rubbed and pinched with loving zest
That roguish feature numbed with cold,
As on the beach in Jan. we strolled
Mid icy blasts from north-nor'-west.

That it was red must be confessed,
And that I kissed it I'll attest,
And proudly shout to all: "Behold!
    I wiped her nose!"

She had no handkerchief—she guess'd—
I took out mine; softly caressed
That tender nose of fairest mould,
And kissed it, too! The tale is told.
On this my claim to fame must rest—
    I wiped *Her* nose!

Written 13 January 1915 and sent to Beatrice Ashe. Printed from the car-
bon typescript among O'Neill papers acquired from Agnes Boulton
(YCAL). The original typescript, in the Berg Collection of the New York
Public Library, has one autograph correction.

41. A DREAM OF LAST WEEK

I remember the moon,
    And the silvered dusk
Of the night's high noon —
I was leaving soon —
I remember the moon.
    I cherish the husk.

I remember your face
    So white in the gloom
Of our trysting place;
So sad for a space!
I remember your face.
    I curse at my doom.

I remember your eyes
    Shining thro' the tears
Of those last goodbyes —
Now my spirit dies —
I remember your eyes.
    I hate the long years.

I remember your lips
    And their clinging kiss;
The curve of your hips! —
I am lashed with whips —
I remember your lips.
    I treasure my bliss.

I remember your hair
　　In its disarray
Lured the wistful air. —
Ah God, you are fair! —
I remember your hair.
　　　Give me Yesterday!

I remember your breast,
　　And a purple stain
Where my lips had rest. —
Your Beloved Best! —
I remember your breast.
　　I torture my brain.

I remember my arm
　　Round your naked waist,
The adorable charm
Of your sweet alarm.
I remember my arm.
　　I have had my taste.

I remember my "Bee"
　　And her heart, My Home.
All her witchery
Casts its spell on me,
I remember my Bee
　　As I dream alone.

Written in January 1915 and sent to Beatrice Ashe. Printed from the autograph manuscript in the Berg Collection of the New York Public Library.

42. LAMENT FOR BEATRICE

Ah, but to bring back just one hour
Of all the hours we have known;
But to be gifted with the power
To cheat the Past of one sweet hour!

To hear within your swelling breast
Your heart beat underneath my head;
To lie within your arms and rest
With sleepy kisses on your breast.

To see your love glow in your eyes
Through silken veils of tangled hair;
To trace the soft line of your thighs;
To drink your beauty with my eyes!

To listen to your lyric voice
Murmuring words of tenderness;
To feel my soul of souls rejoice
And thrill with yearning at your voice.

To know again your love of me,
And try to tell my love for you;
To bow in worship at your knee,
And thank God for your love of me!

Written 15 January 1915 and sent to Beatrice Ashe. Printed from the carbon typescript among O'Neill papers acquired from Agnes Boulton (YCAL). Both the carbon and the original typescript in the Berg Collection of the New York Public Library have two manuscript corrections by the author.

43. SPEAKING, TO THE SHADE OF DANTE, OF BEATRICES

"Lo, even I am Beatrice!"
  That line keeps singing in my bean.
I feel the same ecstatic bliss
  As did the fluent Florentine
Who heard the well-known hell-flame hiss.

Dante, your damozel was tall
  And lean and sad—I've seen her face
On many a best-parlor wall—
  I don't think she was such an ace.
She doesn't class with mine at all.

Her eyes were not so large or grey;
  She had no such heart-teasing smile,
Or hair so beautiful; and say,
  I hate to state it, but her style
Would never get her by today.

I'm not denying that your queen
  In your eyes may have been a bear.
You couldn't pull the stuff I've seen
  About her, if she wasn't there—
That soft poetic bull, I mean.

But just to call your rhythmic bluff
  I'll say, before I ring the bell
And kill this roundelay of fluff,
  Like Dante, I'd go plumtoel
For Beatrice—and that's enough!

Printed, under the heading "The Conning Tower," in the *New York Tribune* for 5 July 1915, as by E. O'N.; reprinted in Sanborn & Clark, pp. 118–119, and also under the heading "The Conning Tower," in the *New York Herald Tribune* for 9 March 1935. An earlier version, with title " 'My Beatrice' (Being a few words with that guy Dante who wrote so much junk about his Beatrice)," is preserved in an original typescript, sent to

Beatrice Ashe, in the Berg Collection of the New York Public Library. This version has a number of punctuation and other minor variants, and has the following additional stanza between four and five, variant fifth stanza, and "Envoy":

I wish that I could spiel as well
    As you did! I could fill some space
If I took pen in hand to tell
    The marvel of my Princess' face,
The sweetness of her witching spell

But I am not there with the stuff,
    And so I better ring the bell
On this, my roundelay of fluff.
    Like you, Dante, I'd go to Hell
For Beatrice,—and that's enough!

        Envoy
(Or something of the sort,—just so I can get personal)

I hear thy soft-voiced melody:
    "Even I am *your* Beatrice!"
I feel my soul dissolve in glee,
    I taste the attar of your kiss,
Maybe, My Bee! My Bee, maybe?

44. "BEYOND THE GREAT DIVIDE"

Beyond the Great Divide! Do we not know
  The wonder and the glory of the land
  Which waits us there? Across the arid sand,
The barren wastes of futile days, aglow
With splendor of new joy, red dawns arise
  To welcome us. Our souls implore, command:
"On! On!" but trembling, hand in hand,
  A furtive coward question in our eyes, —

We wait! — Love mocks us with sad scornful tears.
  We wait! — The wine of life dries in the cup.
  We wait! — The feast grows cold, we dare not sup.
We wait! — A sickly conscience goads our fears.
We feel the baleful boredom of the years;
  Our stricken Youth is wrinkled now, and old;
  The crown of vine leaves crumbles into mold;
We wait! — While Life yawns wearily and sneers.

Warm lips against which mine have kissed and sighed,
  Grey gold-flecked eyes which fear to see the goal,
  Cold pulse? I hear the beating of your soul,
A passionate sob of heart unsatisfied.
Awake, O sleeping Princess! Side by side
  Onward with me to win the highest dream!
  On where the watch-fires of the Future gleam,
Where life is real — Beyond the Great Divide!

Written, probably in 1915, and sent to Beatrice Ashe. Printed from a carbon typescript among O'Neill papers acquired from Agnes Boulton (YCAL). The original typescript is in the Berg Collection of the New York Public Library.

45. "THE WOMAN WHO UNDERSTANDS"

Somewhere she waits to make you win
   Your soul in her firm white hands —
Somewhere the Gods have made for you
   The woman who understands.

As the tide went out she found him
   Lashed to a spar of despair —
The wreck of his ship around him,
   The wreck of his dreams in the air —
Found him and loved him and gathered
   The soul of him to her heart;
The soul that had sailed an uncharted sea —
The soul that had thought to win and be free —
   The soul of which she was part;
And there in the dusk she cried to the man:
   "Win your battle — you can — you can!"

Helping and loving and guiding —
   Urging when that was best —
Holding her fears in hiding
   Deep in her quiet breast —
This is the woman who kept him
   True to his standards lost,
When tossed in the storm and stress and strife,
He thought himself through with the game of life
   And ready to pay the cost,
Watching and guarding and whispering still:
   "Win — you can — and I know you will!"

This is the story of ages —
   This is the woman's way —
Wiser than seers or sages,
   Lifting us day by day.

Facing all things with courage
  Nothing can daunt or dim;
Treading life's path wherever it leads —
Lined with flowers or choked with weeds,
  But ever with him — with him.
Guardian, comrade, and Golden Spur,
The men who win are helped by her.

Somewhere she waits, strong in belief,
  Your soul in her firm white hands;
Thank well the Gods when she comes to you —
  The woman who understands.

Written, probably in 1915, and sent to Beatrice Ashe. Printed from the
carbon typescript in the Berg Collection of the New York Public Library.

46. TRIOLET OF MY FLOWER

Sleep on her breast,
  Rose of my heart!
Flower so blest,
Sleep on her breast;
I crave thy rest,
  Alone, apart!
Sleep on her breast,
  Rose of my heart.

Sent with three red roses to Beatrice Ashe in 1915 when she was sick with typhoid. Printed from the original typescript signed "E. G. O.," in the Berg Collection of the New York Public Library.

47.

I had dwelt too long in lives
My ears were dulled with the monotonous humming of bees
And the talk about honey.
I had forgotten the mad resonance of waves!

Glad as the sea
To city-dwellers' eyes —
O my Beloved.

Your body is warm and undulating
As the sand dunes.
Eager with tremulous heat waves
Beneath my kisses
Your passions stretch upward
Their frantic, quivering hands.

I shall come to you
In the delirium of noon.

Laughter of spray
Dancing on exultant wave-crests;
Thoughtful shadows of clouds
Pass with haunting slowness
From horizon to horizon,
From mystery to mystery:
Whimsical dreams of wind
Stirring the sea's face
To a tender smiling;
And the peace of a twilight
When sea and sky
Become one

And are silent
And the first star is born.

These moods of the sea
Are you, my Beloved.

I am only a seagull
Dolefully squawking
When it would sing.

Written in New London in the summer of 1915. Printed from the original
typescript, extensively revised in pencil, among the O'Neill papers (YCAL).
The typescript has lines 8–15 heavily cancelled in pencil and place and
date of composition added in Eugene O'Neill's hand.

48. VILLANELLE TO HIS LADYE IN WHICH YE POORE SCRIBE COMPLAINETH SORELY BECAUSE THE CURSED MEMORY OF THE THOUSAND OTHERS DOTH POISON HIS DREAMS OF HIS BEATRICE

I dream of all your lovers who have wooed
And gained your kiss, and won your subtle smile—
I am but one among a multitude!

Deep in a gloomy revery I brood.
Pain upon pain my anguished fancies pile.
I dream of all your lovers who have wooed.

Alas, so many others knelt and sued
And played each dear device of loving guile!—
I am but one among a multitude!

What jealous visions haunt my sickly mood!
They rasp my heart-strings like a rusty file.
I dream of all your lovers who have wooed.

Into my highest hopes their ghosts intrude—
(I gnash my teeth in truly tragic style)—
I am but one among a multitude!

Pardon, Sweet Bee, if this, my "stuff" be crude;
My Muse is piqued and peeved 'cause all the while
I dream of all your lovers who have wooed—
I am but one among a multitude.

Written, probably in 1915, and sent to Beatrice Ashe. Printed from a carbon typescript among O'Neill papers acquired from Agnes Boulton (YCAL). Another carbon is in the Berg Collection of the New York Public Library. Both typescripts have the same revisions. Authorship is attributed in both to "Knight One Thousand And One." In the Yale carbon the words "Of His Beatrice" in the sub-title are heavily cancelled in pencil.

49. THE STARS

Stars shoot
Over the blinding blaze of shrapnel
Over the torn fields
And the torn bodies;
Like sedate, amusing fireworks
Set off for the laughter
And the wonder of children.
Stars shoot. —
The harmless and kindly stars.

I think the jaded gods,
Bored by the stench and the slaughter,
Are holding carnival
And throwing confetti.

Printed from an original typescript, dated 1915, and with typed address: "38 Washington Square / New York City," among the O'Neill papers (YCAL). This typescript and a typed copy made by Carlotta Monterey O'Neill about 1940, also in the O'Neill papers (YCAL), have a manuscript correction.

50. LAMENT OF A SUBWAYITE

(W[ith]. A[pologies]. to J. Milton)

When I consider the many hours spent
  As suff'ring on the Subway trains I ride,
  And stand, and hang, and vainly seek to hide
My feet beneath the cross seats to prevent
The colored lady tall and corpulent
    Who wheezes with exhaustion at my side
    From crushing them beneath her massive stride
And maiming me before her swift descent —

Great words of fury sputter in my brain
  And I am tempted to cry out in heat
"A seat! A seat! My kingdom for a seat!
    Why should I bend and break beneath the strain?"
Methinks I hear the song the harsh wheels sang:
    "They also pay who only stand and hang"

Written probably in New York in 1915. Printed from a carbon typescript
among O'Neill papers acquired from Agnes Boulton (YCAL). Compare
Milton's sonnet "On His Blindness."

51.

What do you see,
Wan One,
There,
From your bench
In the park?

It is evening,
The sunset is a dab of rouge
On the pallid cheeks
Of day.

It is autumn.
Why do you stare so
At the bare trees
And the dead grass
And the little people?

It is night,
Wan One,
And autumn.
And the day
Is also dead.

Printed from the autograph manuscript, as revised—in 1940?—by Eugene O'Neill, among the O'Neill papers (YCAL). A typed copy made about 1940 by Carlotta Monterey O'Neill has the same manuscript revisions by Eugene O'Neill, who has added place and date of composition: "Hell Hole 1915."

52.

In that last hour
When he lay
His legs crossed,
His arms crossed,
Even his fingers crossed!

Looking at him,
Looking into his eyes
His meaning was the obstinate gleam
Of some star billionaire of distance
Whose eyes are drugged with eternity
Whose belly is full of time,
Whose empty heart is space!

And here we sit!
You and I—
In the Congo of the soul
All the reverberating tom-toms
Of everlasting infancy
Are drumming out the boom-boom-boom—
(The presence of God in one's ear-drums)
Until one's atheism
Shrieks in the Dark
And cowers on a heap of dung
To pray!

Printed from the original typed copy made about 1940 by Carlotta Monterey O'Neill and revised in manuscript by Eugene O'Neill, who has added place and date of composition: "Hell Hole—1915." The typed copy is among the O'Neill papers (YCAL).

53. SILENCE

The earth,   [Morning]
Stripped bare of sound,
Lies at the feet of Silence,
Like a nude whore,
Gross, sentimental, sweaty,
Dreaming of love.

Fronds of the nipa palms,
Grown contemplative,
Where are your rustling caresses,
Your swishing petticoats?
Does the black lagoon
Love your passionless immobility?
　　*　　*　　*
The sky,   [Noon]
Sick with heat,
Swoons into grey.
Far-off in the cool infinite.
The trees huddle together,
Motionless,
Supporting one another.
Overcome by the languor of Silence
Even the smallest leaf—
Is still.
The ferns,
Delicate as the eyelashes
Of a sleeping child,
Droop in pestilential dampness,

Sated
With the smell and the taste
Of Death;
Bored.
The black lagoon,
An ebony eunuch,
Sleeps,
Indifferent
To the sun.

Heat waves,
Sprites of the Silence,
Dance with light feet
On the green scum of stagnation.
Writhing, fantastic, graceful,
Gauzy-winged butterflies
Flying from beloved corruption
To colorless, scentless blossoms —
Ultimate verities!
O do not fly back from Nirvana
With the secret!

    *   *   *

Silence,   [Afternoon]
Pale, ivory-skinned,
A naked nun
With a rosary of great black pearls
Hanging between her breasts, —
Silence
With cool lips kisses me,
And gives me her rosary
Of dead centuries
To play with.

79

I play with them.
I tell the sins
I have imagined in vain.
Silence
Watches me indifferently
With the cruel, virginal eyes
Of One
Who has given her body to many,
Her soul to none.
      *   *   *

Shadows creep from tree to tree,   [Evening]
The river mist wraps me
In a pale blue shroud.
      *   *   *

A breeze,   [Night]
Fetid and warm,
Faintly stirs the tree-tops.
The fronds
Of the brooding nipa palms
Awaken
To tender, whispering confidences.
Ripples
Sigh on the dull, black face
Of the lagoon —
Sound is born again.
      *   *   *

Sound!
My ears tingle with rhythm.
I must shout!
I must scream defiance!

"Love! Love! Love!"
I cry.
The frightened breeze
Hides in the forest.
My pitiful clamor dies.
All is still.
Not even the echo of my joy
Comes back to me.

Silence!

Printed from the typed copy made probably about 1940 from the original autograph manuscript, extensively revised, dated "7/9/16." The typed copy also has extensive revisions, apparently made by Eugene O'Neill about 1940, radically altering the original line division and cancelling several lines. The time indications of the manuscript are not copied, one misreading ("maddest" for "smallest" in line 21) is not corrected, and the fourth line from the end ("All is still.") is omitted. Both autograph manuscript and typed copy are among the O'Neill papers (YCAL).

54. THE WHITE NIGHT

Tinkle, tinkle, tinkle!
Tinkling ice in the glasses,
Tinkling laughter of little lusts,
Tinkling tinny souls
Of a little man
And a little woman
Dancing to a tinkling tune.

Wine, wine, red wine!
O Nightingale!
O Rose!

Snores,
And the fetid breathing
Of a little man
And a little woman
Commingling
In the dawn.

Printed from the original typed copy made by Carlotta Monterey O'Neill
about 1940 among the O'Neill papers (YCAL). Eugene O'Neill has added
place and date of composition: "Hell Hole — 1916."

55.

Dirty
Bricks
Of buildings!
Sallow
Window shades!
Even the cats
Yowl
For freedom
From their backyards.

Underdrawers
On the lines
Between
Firescapes
Loose their
Evanescent
Charm.

Ah, Love
Indecent,
Beautiful,
How I miss you!

Printed from the original typed copy made by Carlotta Monterey O'Neill
about 1940 among the O'Neill papers (YCAL). Eugene O'Neill has added
place and date of composition: "Hell Hole—1916."

56. GOOD NIGHT

Put out the light!
Let us sleep!
Pull down the shade
Let us hide
From the meaning wink
Of the worldly stars
From the smirk
Of the sated moon
Peering
There
Through the window pane
Dirty with the tears
Of old rains.

Patter, patter, patter,
Go the little feet
Of the little people —
Bound whither?

Chatter, chatter, chatter
Runs the little talk
Of the little people
As they lie
To each other.

Put out the light
Let us sleep!

Printed from an original typescript among the O'Neill papers (YCAL),
revised in pencil by Eugene O'Neill, who has added the date of composi-
tion: "—1916." There is also a typed copy made by Carlotta Monterey
O'Neill about 1940, with Eugene O'Neill's manuscript note: "Hell Hole
—1916." Three lines cancelled in the original typescript do not appear in
the typed copy, but one word (describing the smirk in line 7 as "aenemic")
is deleted in both.

57. REVOLUTION

Tiger, tiger!
How beautiful you look!
How strong you seem!
How somnolent you are!

Have you tested the bars of your cage,
Have you found them too strong,
Is that why you doze?

See the crowds watching you
With their timid, curious eyes!

Tiger, tiger!
You are proud of your stripes
But are you a tiger
Or merely an overgrown .
Alley cat?

Printed from the autograph manuscript, as revised, dated (later): "Hell
Hole 1916." The original title "Tiger" has been cancelled. An earlier
manuscript version appears in the left half of the same leaf. These manu-
scripts are among the O'Neill papers (YCAL).

58. MOONLIGHT

Silver spider,
Brooding
On the blue wall of the infinite,
What passion makes you pale?

You have caught the stars
In your web of moonbeams.
You have sucked from them
Their vibrant scintillations.
Now they hang enmeshed,
Cosmic gnats,
Bloodless,
Still trembling a little.

What passion makes you pale?
The sea loves you.
She has hushed
All the dancing waves to sleep
That she may yearn for you
In solitude.
She has forbidden the wind
To caress even the tiniest ripple,
That you may gloat
Upon your image in her heart
Undisturbed.

What passion makes you pale?
The mute adoration of the world
Guards
Your malevolent serenity.

Are you pale
With the weariness of watching
Love,
The Eater and the Eaten,
Loathsome spider?

Printed from the original typescript among the O'Neill papers (YCAL).
Eugene O'Neill has added (at a later date) a manuscript note: "P'town—
Summer 1916." There is a probable echo from Shelley's "Fragment: To
the Moon": "Art thou pale for weariness / Of climbing Heaven and
gazing on the earth."

59. SUBMARINE

My soul is a submarine.
My aspirations are torpedoes.
I will hide unseen
Beneath the surface of life
Watching for ships,
Dull, heavy-laden merchant ships,
Rust-eaten, grimy galleons of commerce
Wallowing with obese assurance,
Too sluggish to fear or wonder,
Mocked by the laughter of waves
And the spit of disdainful spray.

I will destroy them
Because the sea is beautiful.

That is why I lurk
Menacingly
In green depths.

Printed in the *Masses* for February 1917, unsigned; reprinted in Sanborn & Clark, p. 120, in Gelb, *O'Neill*, p. 321, and in Louis Sheaffer, *O'Neill: Son and Playwright*, pp. 180–181.

60. EYES

I gazed in the mirror
And smiled at myself—
But my eyes could not smile.
They were dead souls,
Imprisoned.
How could they smile?

Yet I must meet her—
And so I shaved,
Shuddering
At the horror
In the mirror.

And a little later
I met her at the train,
And kissed her,
And smiled —
But my eyes could not smile.

I longed to close them.
Why could they not smile?

And her eyes,
Eager with the desire of love,
Stared accusingly;
Then filled with tears
When they saw
The dead.

Printed from a typed copy made about 1940 by Carlotta Monterey O'Neill. Eugene O'Neill has made a correction and has added in manuscript place and date of composition: "N.Y. / Garden Hotel 1917." The O'Neill papers (YCAL) contain also an original typed copy, and an autograph copy of the poem made by Mrs. O'Neill in Boston in 1954.

61. 'TIS OF THEE

This game
Of blind man's buff
Where hatred distils
In synthetic drops of love
Where the grotesque
In the intensity of its becoming,
Blindfold, tags Beauty.

Over tin roofs
The eternal tin cans
Wrapped in the tinfoil of lights
Tinkle in tiny tintillations —
But in the mysticism of my loathing
They are great hypnotic drums
Summoning us cannibals
To an ultimate occasion.

These buildings scrape the sky
With a relentless itch against color
Frozen grey phalluses
In a world that chatters belief
In monkey glands.
Our God snickers like a Methodist preacher
Picking the lock of Darwin's laboratory
To make moonshine out of worms.
Yet from it all, deep rhythm
Frankenstein learning the truth of his childhood
Growing older than his maker's inhibitions
Hearing the pulse of his rivets
Beat in the womb to the heart of his mother
Who dances white nude in the Congo.

But who shall say this?
Not I — One, perhaps, a son of Frankenstein
One who can sing the fire
With lips of furnaces
One who can be a Phoenix
Disdaining rebirth
For the greater meaning of living.

Not I; let me but sing my masochistic song
I will be: Yankee St. Lawrence —
On the grid iron of Old Glory!

Printed from the typed copy made about 1940 by Carlotta Monterey
O'Neill (YCAL). Eugene O'Neill has revised this copy in pencil and ink,
cancelling the original first line: "And I have penetrated the disguise of
Thor in the Harlequin of George M. Cohan." and the final seven lines:

But when I ask you as a lover
Turn me over — Know I am hearing
This hideous hymn reborn within
The barrel-organ of ten million children's wombs —

My country, 'tis of Thee
Sweet land of Liberty
Of Thee I sing.

Added in pencil are place and date of composition: "Hell Hole 1917."

62.

The golden oranges in the patio dream of the Hesperides. The earth is a sun-struck bee, its wings sodden with golden pollen, sifted dust of sunbeams. Dark in the hacienda—the cool hands of a mystic consummation gentle on one's forehead. Life creeps fiercely toward death—but silently—one is aware but does not hear.

Then green parrots in the green of the orange trees gossiping like deaf people—a discord rasps saw-teeth in the keen blue blade of silence——

This memory—the feverish sigh of dying leaves—a hot exhalation of decay from the grave-pocked earth—and the hiding Past steps from behind its tree full in my path—one-fifth of a second—is gone.

Parrots of the past in forgotten orange trees! But the Parrots ye have always with you. The walls of solitude crumble before their strident prophecies. O Jerico of Ours, also conquered by spiders—harmless, not to be found guilty—industrious demons of well-meaning activity spinning their personal connotations in all our favorite shadows! How can we walk in our garden, Thou and I? The webs drift on our eyelids. Blinking, how can we hold each other's eyes? We must eternally scratch the itch from our profaned nakedness.

*   *   *

Gray, blind sphynxes robed in wrinkled sand-shrouds. Here in a mirrored gesture of tired pain one senses the stiffened flexing of claws weary with time, too old to desire death. The sea bathes their feet in green, sacrificial wine and chants a querulous hymn under her breath—or raging at the bruised question in their buried eyes, flecks their flanks with her disdainful spittle, maddened by her passion's own obscurity. But they are inviolate, beyond the hope of any further dream; and in dim sanctuaries underground their worshippers, the dead, are born and die again.

*   *   *

O sea, which is myself! How I love to reveal my nakedness to the sun on solitary beaches! How I love to play unconsciously, dancing like another heat-wave to its own rhythm, freed from the fretting, lukewarm glance of human eyes! And after the rippling laughter of teasing wind, the warm yielding kinship of sand which moulds my own image, to relax and drown in my silent depths deep in the heart of steadfast, simple tides flowing from eternity to eternity as the cloud shadows march across the world from mystery to mystery.

I lie in the profound half-light of some old grotto sacred to myself, and the moon-eyed fishes which are my thoughts peer in one by one and drift wistfully away, and the great currents of being sweep around making my skin quiver with the caress of subtle emotions which kiss and are ever unseen.

And then suddenly there is warmth and light and the blossoming of spring flowers on the floor of the sea—and a song which is a tantalizing secret and a murmur of revelation—and You are there! And you walk serenely in the great depths of me with dear, familiar gestures as one who is at home and does not know—how strange home is! And the moon-eyed fishes which are my thoughts attend you like pensioners; and the great tides of my life would offer you their arms like eager courtiers and smooth your way; and the currents of my soul are slim fingers dressing your hair with gifts.

*   *   *

And then I remember of old time that a great hush of nonbeing was the portent of your approach. And I know that I never was I, and am not, and cannot be; and I see by the smile in your eyes that you never were you, and are not, and cannot be!

Life ever the expression of other life—never separate—the futile dead which are You and I—unwept, reborn, transfigured to meaning in We—and passed on————

Printed from a typescript, dated September 1919, among O'Neill papers acquired from Agnes Boulton (YCAL). The date "September 1919" is added in pencil in an unidentified hand.

63. TO ALICE

The sun
And you
Two things in life
Are true.

Two things are true.
You are one.
Your hair
And the sun.

Your eyes
And the sea
Innocence
And liberty.

Rusty chains
Eat the soul
We are wise
But you are whole

You, the sun, & sea,
Trinity!
Sweet spirit, pass on
Keep the dream
Beauty
Into infinity.

Written, probably in 1925 in Bermuda, to a young woman with whom
Eugene O'Neill used to swim. Printed from the autograph manuscript
in the Clifton Waller Barrett Collection, University of Virginia Library.

64. INTERLUDE

And so
We strolled sadly into a Tomorrow—
Rather a dim land
So empty and contented—
All dreams had become
Soiled and true
And yawned themselves to death!

And Nero said to me:
"Oh yes, my mother was a good woman
And I only killed her because—
(How vague time makes one!)—well,
Because she had a wart on her chin
And because I was God!
Don't you think it's a bit degrading of God
To have a mother?
One must do something about it."

And he fell asleep again.
I turned to Caligula
Who whispered perversely
"I once had a horse
A milk-white horse
And I fed him on gilded oats
From a golden manger
In a stall of ivory—
But he never grew wings—"
(This Son of God said sadly—)
"He never became Pegasus
He was just a fat, white horse
And I finally gave him to the Circus
Where he was eaten by a flea-bitten lion."

"Life is strange," (Caligula sighed.)
Now I am dead I sometimes think that Fate
Is a fat white horse

Time wrung the dirty diapers of dawn—
(One sometimes half suspects
That Allah, the Merciful,
Wears flannel underwear!)
A ghost that was Domitian sidled up
And we shook wings
For we were both so dead!
So dead and lucid!
He said:
"If you'll remember
A silly soothsayer once told me
I'd be stabbed in the back
So I put mirrors on every wall
And nobody came behind me
That I couldn't see.
Yet,"—(and his rheumy eyes grew startled)
"Someone did
And stabbed me in the back—
It's hell to live in a world of mirrors," he said
"The murderer was—
The assassin was—
Well—hmm—never mind
You'll have to prove me guilty"
And he dove into a lake of flame
To escape from Hell!

There are so many afternoons
Afternoon—and afternoon—and afternoon—
One sits and reflects
There is music in one's ear—

Discordant music—
As the golden strings
Are plucked broken from the harp of youth
One by one, and every one the last!
Before one's meager eyes
The stark horizons of the past and future
Expand like rubber bands,
Gaping to contract on one's heart
Until the cosmos is barred rays of light
Through which one's faint-eyed soul
Stares like an orphan out of a book.

Written probably in 1925 in Bermuda. Printed from the original autograph manuscript in the Clifton Waller Barrett Collection, University of Virginia Library.

65.

How weary we are!
We scarce can drag one thought after another
Up the long tiresome hill to Calvary
To keep our tryst
With Thou and the two thieves;
Where now they crucify us all
On question marks,
And that man there,
And this man here,
Who beats his brain against a rock,
And I myself
We all are Lazarus
And we accuse Thee!

Yea, standing on that hill
That man and this man and I
We stretch our arms defenceless to the sky
We are the Emperor and the crucified
We are the hunter — and the kill!

Oh Jehovah, I hope your bosom is as hairy
As ten Ostermoors!
For I am awfully tired, Daddy,
And I deserve sleep!

Written in Bermuda, 3 May 1925. Printed from the original untitled autograph manuscript, initialed and dated, in the Clifton Waller Barrett Collection, University of Virginia Library.

66. QUIET SONG IN TIME OF CHAOS
To Carlotta on Her Birthday

Here
Is home.
Is peace.
Is quiet.

Here
Is love
That sits by the hearth
And smiles into the fire,
As into a memory
Of happiness,
As into the eyes
Of quiet.

Here
Is faith
That can be silent.
It is not afraid of silence.
It knows happiness
Is a deep pool
Of quiet.

Here
Sadness, too,
Is quiet.
Is the earth's sadness
On autumn afternoons
When days grow short,
And the year grows old,

When frost is in the air,
And suddenly one notices
Time's hair
Has grown whiter.

Here?
Where is here?
But you understand.
In my heart
Within your heart
Is home.
Is peace.
Is quiet.

Written at Christmastime 1940 for Carlotta's birthday, 28 December 1940. Printed from the autograph manuscript, signed "Gene / Christmas 1940," among the O'Neill papers (YCAL). The manuscript is reproduced with a transcript in *Inscriptions: Eugene O'Neill to Carlotta Monterey O'Neill,* privately printed in New Haven in 1960.

67. FRAGMENTS

So am I isolate,
Inviolate,
Untouchable,
Bitterest of all, ungivable,
Unable to bestow,
Break from my solitude
A lonely gift,
Myself.

Oh, I have tried to scream!
Give pain a voice!
Make it a street singer
Acting a pantomime of tragic song,
To beg the common copper
Of response:
An ear
To hear.

But something was born wrong.
The voice
Strains toward a sob.
Begins and ends in silence.

How can they hear
That cry denied an utterance?
Or see,
Staring at me,
Whose eyes are blindly silent.

For seemingly
I am a quiet man,

Unmoved,
Objective,
Without much feeling
Hiding within a crevice
Of the mind.

How can they see the tear,
Born dry and never shed,
Or pity the dream?
Oh well, I will dream anew:
I will hope
There is communion
Among the dead.

Oh, I have tried to pray
In simple faithlessness!
Ground my bloody knees
Into the stone!

(Not my real knees,
You understand,
They cannot kneel.)

I have cried beseechingly
"O God!"

(Silently,
You understand,
Because I am a quiet man
Who longs for quiet,
Seemingly,
As I have said.)

"O God!
O Universal Life!
O Cosmic Reproduction!"

(Any name will do
When all names
Are but names.)

"O, Anything-At-All
Above,
Beyond,
Hidden behind,
Or locked within,
O harken to the prayer
I cannot pray —
My humble prayer!"

(As if sick pride
Could climb the mountain top,
Humility.)

The echoes die,
Unrequitedly.
(A figure of speech,
You understand.
There are no echoes.)

All this,
As I have said before,
Happens where silence is;
Where I,
A quiet man,
In love with quiet,
Live quietly
Among the visions of my drowned,
Deep in my silent sea.

Written at Tao House, Danville, California, 17 August 1942. A typed copy made from the autograph manuscript by Carlotta Monterey O'Neill was extensively revised by the author on 15 May 1944. A typed copy of the revised version was prepared by Mrs. O'Neill, presumably in 1944, and was itself revised in manuscript by Eugene O'Neill. The text used here is that of a typed copy of this revised typescript, which has a few further manuscript revisions by the author. Other typed copies made by Carlotta Monterey O'Neill exist. There is also a copy in pencil by Mrs. O'Neill, and an ink copy made by her in Boston, 8 July 1954. All these versions are in the O'Neill papers (YCAL).

68. FRAGMENTS

I am a quiet man
Who longs for solitude
Ostensibly.
Pursues—frantically
Even in doctors' offices
Wa[i]ting, feeling old
As outdated as the magazines.
Then admitted to the Presence:
"Oh, Doctor, I am sick."
"You?"
The smile is kindly,
"Evidently something is sick,
Your brain, perhaps,
Or stomach,
Or kidneys
Or nerves.
Yes, I can see you're nervous
The mind, too
We cure even that nowadays.
Medical science has progressed.
It gives the mind answers
Which, unfortunately, stubborn cases
Insist are only further questions."
"Oh, Doctor, perhaps it is
The soul."
"The soul?"
The smile still kindly
But now a little amused
Thinly concealing condescension.
"Oh, it's your soul
That bothers you, is it?"

"Yes, Doctor, I lie awake
There is no sleep
I suffer torments."
"Here's a prescription,
A harmless barbiturate.
Your trouble is common enough:
It's the war.
Everyone has the jitters."

Exit, bearing pills.

Written 17 August 1942 at Tao House, Danville, California. Printed from
the autograph pencil manuscript, written on the recto of the third of
four leaves, of which the first two bear the manuscript of the preceding
"Fragments," and the final leaf has No. 69. Each leaf is headed "Frag-
ments" and each is numbered in the upper-right corner. These manu-
scripts are in the O'Neill papers (YCAL), which contain no typed copies of
this part of the poem.

69. FRAGMENTS

The War?
Oh, you mean the present symptoms
Of spiritual disease.
It's nothing new.
My generation,
The aged middle-aged,
Were born as the slow dying
Began in earnest:
The scientific murder of the spirit.
We have spent our lives
Slowly dying
For one liberty,
Freedom from the spirit.
We have spent our lives
Contriving our own assassination.
This war is old.
We are the enemy.
He is our logical mistake.
We made him what he is.
He is our wish,
Free man,
Emancipated
From the shackles of the soul.
An animal with brains.

And so
Let us go on
To victory!
Which is once more
Defeat!

A peace
Which will again betray
Those silent men,
The dead.

Written 17 August 1942 at Tao House, Danville, California. The auto-
graph manuscript of the first section of the poem, a manuscript in the
hand of Carlotta Monterey O'Neill of the second section, three typed
copies made by her, the last with Eugene O'Neill's manuscript revisions,
made probably in 1944, are all in the O'Neill papers (YCAL). The text is
that of the revised typed copy. There is also a manuscript copy of the
first section made by Mrs. O'Neill in Boston on 8 July 1954.

70. FRAGMENTS

Through indolence,
Irony,
Helplessness, too, perhaps,
He let the legends go,
The lying legends grow;
Then watched the mirror darken,
Indolently,
Ironically,
Helplessly, too, perhaps,
Until one final day
Only a ghost remained
To haunt its shallow depths—
Himself,
Bewildered apparition,
Seeking a lost identity.

Written 10 September 1942 at Tao House, Danville, California. An autograph draft in pencil by the author, four typed copies made by Carlotta Monterey O'Neill (two with manuscript corrections by Eugene O'Neill), and a final typed copy incorporating the revisions are in the O'Neill papers (YCAL). The text used is that of the final typed copy. It was printed, without title, in Louis Sheaffer, *O'Neill: Son and Artist.* (Boston, Toronto, Little, Brown and Co. [1973]), p. 534.

71. FRAGMENT

Suggested by newspaper article about old woman arrested
for drunkenness Dec. '42

Drunk?
Yes, I was drunk.
I'm an old lady now, you see,
I'm ninety-two.
That's very old.
That's very old, you know.

My husband died
Sixteen long years ago.
I loved him, you see.

Those have been long, long years.

So
To take up time,
To fill the empty, lonely time,
I started sipping wine.

And when I've sipped a lot
I ride the street cars
Night and day,
Up and down,
To nowhere,
Just to pass the time.
When I get tired,
And it's cold,
As it was cold last night
I sleep in a park
Wrapped in newspapers.

At times
I get very cold
But I don't mind
For you get used to cold
When for long, long years
You have been waiting,
Passing the time
Growing too old.

Written, presumably in December 1942, at Tao House, Danville, California. Printed from the autograph manuscript among the O'Neill papers (YCAL).

72. SONG IN CHAOS

For Carlotta

What if the world be mad?
You are near.
What if the mind be sad?
You are here
In my heart,
My dear.

What if the dream grow old
In a world of fear?
What if the spirit be cold?
You are here
In my heart,
My dear.

Love is not mad nor sad.
Love is not old nor cold.
Love is here,
In my heart,
For you,
My dear.

Written for Carlotta Monterey O'Neill's birthday, 28 December 1942, at Christmastime 1942. Printed from the original signed typescript, made by Carlotta Monterey O'Neill, among the O'Neill papers (YCAL). An autograph version incorporated in a letter to Carlotta, Christmas 1942, was reproduced, with transcript, in *Inscriptions: Eugene O'Neill to Carlotta Monterey O'Neill*, privately printed in New Haven in 1960.

INDEX

Arabic numerals refer to numbers assigned to poems

"Ah, but to bring back just one hour" 42
"All night I lingered at the Beach" 7
Amundsen, Roald 15
"And so / We strolled . . ." 64
"As I scan the pages of history's scroll" 13
Ashe, Beatrice 33–46, 48

"Ballade of Old Girls" 5
"Ballade of the Birthday of the Most Gracious of Ladyes" 30
"Ballade of the Modern Music Lover" 12
"Ballade of the Seamy Side" 27
"'Ballade of the Two of Us'" 38
Barrett, Clifton W. v, 63–64
Becker, Charles 3
Beinecke Rare Book and Manuscript Library vii, 1. *See also*
    Yale Collection of American Literature.
Berg Collection v, vii, 31, 34–43, 45–46, 48
"'Beyond the Great Divide'" 44
"'Blow, blow thou winter wind'" 29
Boston Red Sox 10
Boulton, Agnes v, 35–38, 40, 42–43, 48, 50, 62
"Braw, snortin', roarin', fearsome beastie" 8
Burns, Robert vii, 8

"The Call" 24
"The call resounds on every hand" 32
Clark, Barrett vii, 12, 15
Clark, Mary A. 30
Cohan, George M. 61
"The Conning Tower" 43
Cook, Frederick A. 29
Crane, Joan St.C. vii

Davenport, William H. v
"Dirty / Bricks" 55
"A Dream of Last Week" 41
"Drunk? / Yes, I was drunk" 71

"The earth" 53
"Eyes" 60

Floyd, Virginia vii
"For the Waterways Convention's in the Morning" 2

"Fragment" 71
"Fragments" 67–70
"Fratricide" 32
"Free" 1
"'Full Many a Cup of This Forbidden Wine'" 35

Gelb, *O'Neill* 1, 14, 17, 20, 24, 29, 32, 59
"The Glints of Them" 19
"The golden oranges . . ." 62
"Good Night" 56
"Grey sky and a road by the sea" 39
Gyp the Blood 3

Hammond, Edward C. 34
Harkness 34
"The Haymarket" 25
"He fights where the fighting is thickest" 22
"Here / Is home" 66
"Hitting the Pipe" 20
Horowitz, Harry 3
"How weary we are!" 65

"I am a quiet man" 68
"I dream of all your lovers who have wooed" 48
"I gazed in the mirror" 60
"I had dwelt too long in lives" 47
"I have eaten my share of 'stock fish'" 24
"I have tried to fall for the stuff of Mozart" 12
"I might forget the subway guard" 9
"I remember the moon" 41
"I used to ponder deeply o'er" 10
"I wandered the wide world over . . ." 18
"I wiped her nose . . ." 40
"I wrote a sonnet to her eyes" 21
"Impression" 39
"In that last hour" 52
Inscriptions 66, 72
"'It's Great When You Get In'" vi, 15

"'Just a Little Love, A Little Kiss'" 36
"'Just Me n' You'" 37

Kipling, Rudyard vii, 2, 16, 23, 31
Knight One Thousand and One 48

"Laconics" 3–29
"Lady accept this feeble rhyme" 30

"Lament for Beatrice" 42
"Lament of a Subwayite" 50
"Laughing gilt laden did they come to me" 19
"The Lay of the Singer's Fall" 28
Lefty Louie 3
"List to the lure of my arguments" 31
"'Lo, even I am Beatrice!'" 43
"The Long Tale" 23
Longfellow, Henry W. 3
"Love's Lament" 17

Mahanus 3
Marquard, Rube 10
Mason, Walt vii, 18
Masses 59
Mathewson, Christy 10
Milton, John 50
"Moonlight" 58
Murray, Katherine 31
"The music blares into a ragtime tune" 25
"My Beatrice" 43
"My soul is a submarine" 59

New London Public Library vii
New London Telegraph v, vi, 2–29
New York Call 32
New York Giants 10
New York Herald Tribune 43
New York Public Library v. *See also* Berg Collection.
New York Tribune 43
"Nocturne" vi. 11
"Noon" 26

"O the conning and the bulling!" 3
Omar Khayyám 34, 36
O'Neill, Carlotta M. v, vii, 1, 33, 49, 51–52, 54–56, 60–61, 66–67, 69–70, 72
O'Neill papers 1. *See also* Yale Collection of American Literature.
"Only You" vi, 14
"Our Teddy opens wide his mouth" 6
"Outside the rattling flat-wheeled cars roll by" 36

Peary, Robert E. 15, 29
Pleiades Club Year Book 1
"Put out the light!" 56

"'The Quest of the Golden Girl'" 18
"Quiet Song in Time of Chaos" 66

"A Regular Sort of a Guy"   22
"Revolution"   57
Riley, James W.   6, 20, 38
"Rondeau: To Her Nose"   40
Roosevelt, Theodore   6
Rosenberg, Louis   3
Rosenthal, Herman   3

Sanborn & Clark, *Bibliography*   v, 1, 3–14, 16–29, 32, 43, 59
Scott, Maibelle   1, 4, 14, 17
"Sentimental Stuff"   21
Service, Robert W.   vii
"Sez the wily campaign manager"   16
Sheaffer, Louis   vi, vii, 25, 34, 59, 70
"The Shut-Eye Candidate"   16
"Silence"   53
"Silver spider"   58
"A singer was born in a land of gold"   28
"Sleep on her breast"   46
"So am I isolate"   67
"Somewhere she waits to make you win"   45
"Song in Chaos"   72
"A Song of Moods"   33
"Sonnets"   25–26
Speaker, Tris   10
"Speaking, to the Shade of Dante, of Beatrices"   43
"The Stars"   49
"Stars shoot"   49
"Submarine"   59
"The sun / And you"   63
"The sunset gun booms out in hollow roar"   11
Szladits, Lola   vii

Taft, William H.   3, 6
Tesreau, Jeff   10
Thaw, Harry K.   3
"There ain't no nothing much no more"   17
"There's a speech within the hall . . ."   23
"They told me the water was lovely"   15
"This game"   61
"Through indolence / Irony"   70
"Tiger"   57
"Tinkle, tinkle, tinkle!"   54
"'Tis noon . . ."   26
"'Tis of Thee"   61
"To a Bull Moose"   8

"To Alice" 63
"To sing the charms of Rosabelle" 4
"To winter" 29
"Triolet of My Flower" 46

"Upon Our Beach" 34

"Villanelle . . ." 4
"Villanelle to His Ladye . . ." 48
Villon, François vii, 4
Virginia, University of, Library v, vii, 63–64

"The wan beams fret upon the shadowed floor" 35
"The War?" 69
Waterways Convention 2–3
"The Waterways Convention: A Study in Prophecy" 3
"We walk down this crowded city street" 14
"Weary am I of the tumult . . ." 1
"We're outward bound for the Land of Dreams" 37
"What do you see" 51
"What if the world be mad?" 72
"When I consider the many hours spent" 50
"When my dreams come true . . ." 20
"When our dreams come true" 38
"When the sun sprites play . . ." 33
"Where is Cora the corn-fed girlie?" 5
"Where is the lure of the life you sing?" 27
"The White Night" 54
Whitten vii
"'Why are the flags all hanging out?'" 2
"'The Woman Who Understands'" 45
Wood, Joe 10

Yale Collection of American Literature vii, 1–2, 30, 35–38, 40, 42–43, 47–58, 60, 62, 66–72
Yale University vii
"Ye Disconsolate Poet to His 'Kitten' . . ." 31